Anchorman

Bruce Graham

Pottersfield Press, Lawrencetown Beach, Nova Scotia, Canada

Library and Archives Canada Cataloguing in Publication

Graham, Bruce
Anchorman

ISBN 978-1-897426-03-6

1. Graham, Bruce. 2. Television news anchors – Canada – Biography.
3. Television journalists – Canada – Biography. 4. Radio journalists – Canada – Biography.
I. Title.
PN1992.4.G69A3 2008 070.92 C2008-903207-1

Cover design by Gail LeBlanc

Pottersfield Press acknowledges the financial support of the Government of Canada through the Book Publishing Industry Development Program for our publishing activities. We acknowledge the ongoing support of the Canada Council for the Arts, which last year invested $20.1 million in writing and publishing throughout Canada. We also thank the Province of Nova Scotia for its support through the Department of Tourism, Culture and Heritage.

Pottersfield Press
83 Leslie Road
East Lawrencetown, Nova Scotia, Canada, B2Z 1P8
Website: www.pottersfieldpress.com
To order phone toll-free 1-800-NIMBUS9 (1-800-646-2879)
Printed in Canada

Canada

The Canada Council for the Arts · Le Conseil des Arts du Canada

NOVA SCOTIA
Tourism, Culture and Heritage

Contents

Prologue

Orange, gold and green mingled with slashes of crimson covered the mountainside. Corn stalks had lost all sense of summer, their leaves stiff and brittle. The grass had a crunch when you stepped on it. My cameraman was grabbing a final shot before we raced back to the other farm at the cusp of the Annapolis Valley. The competition was keen between the giants of the pumpkin patch. Two men were trying not only to grow the world's biggest pumpkin but to set a new world record. A controversy had started to simmer when reigning champ, Howard Dill, accused Owen Woodman of growing something other than a pumpkin. Was that great gourd in Woodman's garden a giant squash? Would Woodman be disqualified from the world championship of giants? Standing in the autumn sun, Owen Woodman was not much higher than his contender as he defended the heritage of his gourd.

We had great interviews from Dill and Woodman and fantastic shots of the fields, farms and rolling hills in the blush of autumn. It wasn't an earth-shaking story. No doubt in Ottawa reporters would think their pieces much more important. But mine was a story people would pay attention to and talk about while the daily detritus of the capital was forgotten. My story featured men of the soil, faces furrowed by the sun. Nothing phony here, just a rivalry over the tricky difference between a giant pumpkin and a giant squash. When they're both monsters of several hundred pounds, the difference to the naked eye is indistinguishable.

I would be back on the anchor desk in a few hours, my story edited and scripted, and I would relay it to the audience as an anchorman in a shirt and tie. But I had spent the day under the blue sky surrounded by the rainbow on the hills interviewing honest men of the land. Tomorrow I would be somewhere else, talking to other people about other things and I wondered if anyone anywhere ever had a better job.

My life as a broadcaster and anchorman is not an autobiography or an unofficial history of the last half-century. It is a rich medley of life experiences, observations, commentaries and occasional input from viewers who took it upon themselves to correct or contradict me in my nightly rambling on various aspects of the news. I realized while starting to research this book I've done a lot of living – from dangerous streets in Boston to dangerous people in the Middle East; from pushing for television cameras in the Nova Scotia Legislature to laughing over beer with Ralph Kline.

I covered stories that range from politics to pumpkins but it was always the audience that made the job great. I never felt I was talking into a vacuum. This book is dedicated to the radio listeners and television viewers to let them know I'm still kicking and hope they are too.

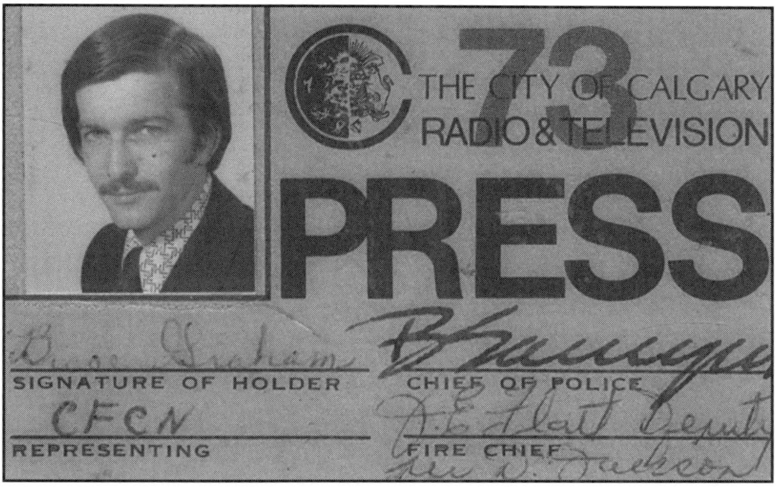
73
THE CITY OF CALGARY
RADIO & TELEVISION
PRESS
SIGNATURE OF HOLDER
CHIEF OF POLICE
CFCN
REPRESENTING
FIRE CHIEF

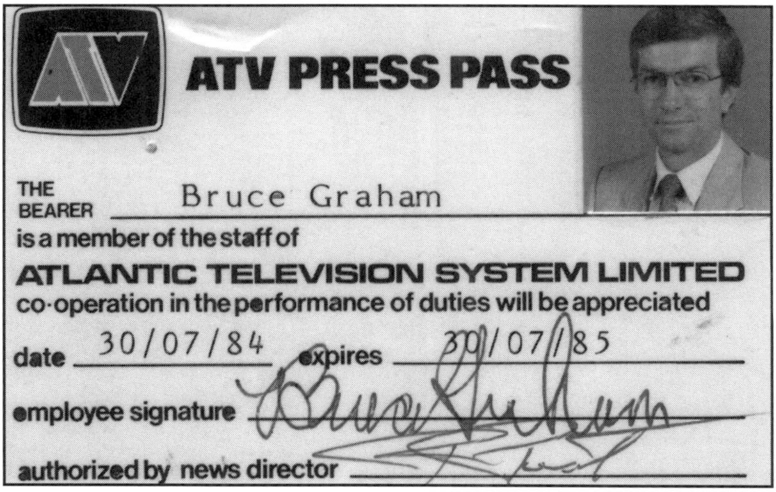
ATV PRESS PASS
THE BEARER Bruce Graham
is a member of the staff of
ATLANTIC TELEVISION SYSTEM LIMITED
co-operation in the performance of duties will be appreciated
date 30/07/84 expires 30/07/85
employee signature
authorized by news director

NEW BRUNSWICK BROADCASTING CO., LIMITED
mitv
This is to certify that:
Bruce Graham
is a staff member of MITV News Department
New Brunswick Broadcasting Co., Limited
EXPIRY DATE:
31 1 92
AUTHORIZATION
NEWS DIRECTOR
EMPLOYEE SIGNATURE

PRESS – PRESSE
VISIT OF / VISITE DU
PRIME MINISTER INDIRA GANDHI
PREMIER MINISTRE, Mme INDIRA GANDHI
GRAHAM, Bruce
CTV and NEWS RADIO
ACCREDITATION OFFICER/AGENT D'ACCREDITATION
NON TRANSFERABLE/NON TRANSMISSIBLE

ROYAL VISIT 1979 VISITE ROYALE
Visit of — Visite de
Her Majesty Queen Elizabeth The Queen Mother
Sa Majesté la reine Élizabeth la Reine mère
CANADA
MÉDIA
GRAHAM, Bruce
ATV. CJCH-TV. CTV(DNS)
Victor G. Chapman
Media Coordinator
Coordonnateur des média
130

Visite royale
1987
Royal Visit
1987
E
Bruce GRAHAM
ATV
MÉDIAS
MEDIA
Coordonnateur des médias / Media Coordinator

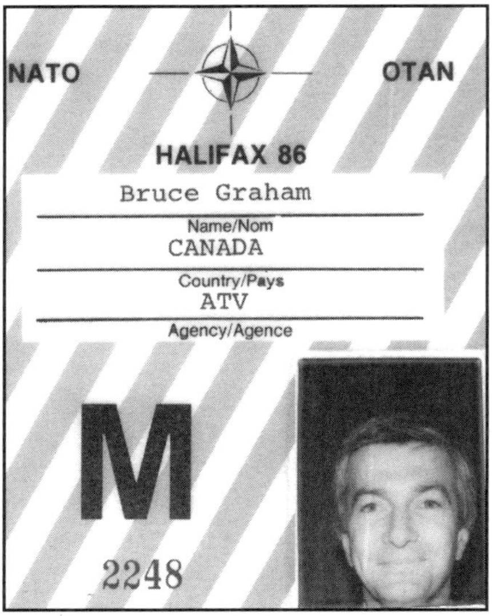
NATO
OTAN
HALIFAX 86
Bruce Graham
Name/Nom
CANADA
Country/Pays
ATV
Agency/Agence
M
2248

1

Halifax, 1962

Romper Room and the Magic Mirror

Finlay MacDonald Sr., the silver-haired owner of CJCH radio and television, walked so fast down the hall, I had trouble just keeping up with him. I was there for a job interview and Finlay was giving me the five-cent tour of radio before turning me over to someone else. He was a man clearly comfortable in his environment, snapping his fingers to the music coming from the control room. If not comfortable myself, at least I dressed for the occasion, wearing my only suit with a white shirt and Nova Scotia tartan tie. I might not have been nearly as natty as MacDonald, but I was overdressed compared to the relaxed attire of the rest of the staff.

A disc jockey named Steve Emery lounged against the wall next to the three short steps to the nerve centre of the radio station – the control room. This is where records were spun, tapes were played and the commercials were read. For a radio station in the 1960s, the control room was the centre of everything. The operator sat between turntables facing a sound mixing board with more dials than a jetliner. That day the operator happened to be Frank Landry from Antigonish. In later years he turned out to be one of my best friends.

From a glass booth, well-known Halifax radio host Bill Fulton was doing his morning show, *Breakfast with Bill*. Records were spinning, machines were whirling, Fulton was talking and to me it all fit together in a fascinating and wondrous coordination that I hardly had time to grasp before I was escorted up to the adjoining television station for my interview. The television offices were the newer and more elaborate part of the building on Robie Street in North End Halifax. Upstairs offices had rich broadloom, better furniture and felt rather subdued after the beat and vibe of radio.

TV manager Dennis Benwell interviewed me and after a pleasant conversation, he rose from his desk and pulled back the drapes on his office wall. Windows looked directly onto the floor of the big television studio. Like giant grey flower heads, huge lights hung haphazardly from the grid. Above the lights was the catwalk, two narrow boards where the studio crews constantly changed, adjusted and fine-tuned the lighting several times a day. Almost all local programs were live in those days and every program required different lighting so a great deal of time was spent on the catwalk. I was asked if I would mind working high off a concrete floor. Certainly not, I replied. It looked safe enough. Nobody wore safety harnesses or hard hats at that time and desperately grabbing one of the lights to break a fall was not an option unless you wanted fried hands as well as a cracked skull. Eager for a job, danger was not a consideration. I saw this as my chance to break into the business and I would have jumped off the catwalk if necessary. My eagerness paid off. I was hired and assigned to one of the two studio crews. I was working in television.

My first task was to become familiar with the mike boom. I would also learn to operate the studio camera, hang lights, lug in boxes of groceries for the commercials, paint flats occasionally and if there was any downtime, clean and repair lights, sweep the floor or anything else that became necessary. I was starting at the bottom, exactly where I deserved to be, but I at least had my foot in the door. My dream of being a television director was a step closer to reality.

There were immediate problems. The first had to do with resentment from some of my fellow workers. There were four men on a studio crew and a crew chief who was responsible for the lighting done by his crew. Lighting was considered an art form and the two crews were in constant competition. Under the crew chief were two camera operators, an audio operator and a mike boom operator – me. The two camera operators on our crew were recent graduates of Ryerson Institute of Technology in Toronto. They had finished a three-year course in radio and television arts, yet my salary of $50 a week equalled their pay and they mightily resented it. A few years my senior, they made no secret of their dissatisfaction. It increased the already considerable friction between the crews that I at first misjudged as keen competition. Within a short space of time I saw it was really petty jealousy. The dissatisfaction of my workmates just added to a volatile mix.

The second problem was the contrariness of the mike boom itself. How difficult could it be to wheel around a tripod holding a twenty-foot-long aluminum boom with a microphone on one end? The boom operator received directions from control through a headset. Sounds simple, or so I thought until I discovered the boom had a mind of its own when it came to which direction it should go. It was not unlike one of those supermarket carts with a rebellious wheel that refuses to be steered – a cart with a twenty-foot-long pole attached to it. That mike boom was a contraption with disaster written all over it. You had to balance the boom and lock it in place because it could drop suddenly. Unfortunately, that was what happened to poor Miss Anne, the erstwhile host of *Romper Room*, the program on which I cut my teeth in television.

Romper Room was unlike any other television program I have ever worked on. It was totally live and full of five-year-old children in the time when television was still a household novelty. If you could stand the pandemonium, *Romper Room* was a good training ground. Anything could happen. The excitable children arrived with full bladders and boundless energy. There were accidents and near accidents and it took a lot of mental agility and quick reflexes on the part of everyone. I didn't have little brothers or sisters, so I knew very little about five-year-olds and just how unpredictable they could be.

As a parent, having a child on *Romper Room* was a big event in 1962. Grandparents and friends were notified so they could see their little loved ones all dressed in their Sunday best on the television. Of course, the children were affected by the family excitement. This contagious nature caused some of the more extroverted to try for a big splash in front of the camera. More than once, a child would suddenly jump up and down in front of the camera or burst into song in the middle of Miss Anne's story. Show business can do that to people.

These occasions always happened when one youngster had an urgent desire for Mother while another would start to cry and grab his crotch while crossing his legs as a sign of severe distress. Things could turn very fast from fun on a wide shot to sudden disaster and tight shots to avoid embarrassments, such as concealing the fact little Johnny was peeing himself while jumping up and down grabbing himself. Miss Anne could be interviewing a child on a wide shot when suddenly the little tike would hike up her dress to show off the new panties Grandma had bought her while another youngster exclaimed loudly on air, "I have to go pee."

Day after day Miss Anne handled such minor instances without acknowledging there was an emergency. The crew and the control room became expert at quick shot changes. The director was constantly on his toes. When Miss Anne was sitting down, I often had to discard my headset and usher a child to waiting parents for a quick bathroom break.

There were fewer commercials in those days and programs weren't peppered with annoying ads as they are today. It was live television in the truest sense. Through it all Miss Anne handled every situation with aplomb. She always kept her cool over the cries, gurgles, burps and other indications of trouble. At times the crew didn't handle things as well. There was a high level of frustration some days when the director screamed for a shot change but the camera operator was off his headset, trying to shuffle children back to their parents. We had a big burly cameraman on our crew from North Bay, Ontario. More than once he walked to the side of his camera that shielded him from the parents to shake his fist at a child who had his hand tightly wedged between his legs, silently crying because he had to go potty. Under the hot lights the odour of urine became extremely unpleasant.

Romper Room ran from 11:30 to 12 noon Monday to Friday, and Miss Anne ended each program by looking into her magic mirror, which gave her the power to see into her vast television land and see the children at home. She would call out various names, particularly if a child had written in to the program or recently won a prize. Some days, I expect due to mental exhaustion, Miss Anne ran out of make-believe names or her magic mirror wasn't working as well so she used the names of the studio crew.

"And there's little Mickey and yes, there is Bruce too and Wayne."

When she did this we would always wave back, delighted at the recognition and relieved the program was almost over.

As the mike boom operator during *Romper Room*, it was my job to follow Miss Anne around the studio as she led the dozen or so children through various games and songs. They would often form a circle and play something like Ring Around the Rosy.

The mortal sin for any boom operator was to get the microphone in the camera shot. This was considered unprofessional and very bad form. When the song and dance portion of *Romper Room* ended, Miss Anne led the children back to her chair and they encircled her as she read them a short story. It was a breather for me because I could lock the boom in place over her and relax until one of the children needed to be taken to their parents.

When I had finally learned to steer the boom and felt comfortable with it, I made my first big mistake. Instead of locking the boom in place where it should have been just out of the camera shot, I accidentally loosened it and the microphone fell straight down, whacking Miss Anne on the noggin. The control room was frantic, shouting orders at me while the two cameramen thought it was hilarious. Miss Anne, being the true professional she was, simply touched the top of her head and said, "Oh! Mr. Mike has come down for a visit."

In every television program, a fault report is kept in the control room. It is the director's diary of the show, including all technical and human mistakes that occurred on the program. On the day I knocked Miss Anne on the head the director wrote, "Miss Anne attacked by Mr. Mike."

On a very hectic program three days later, I became preoccupied and wasn't at my station fast enough as Miss Anne rose from her chair after her story. She struck her head on the microphone that should have been moving upward with her as she got to her feet. The fault report that day read, "Miss Anne strikes back."

I learned a lot from Anne Ramey. She was a consummate

professional in every sense of the word. She could handle any on-air crisis and there always seemed to be one. Not only did she host *Romper Room* five days a week, she also produced and hosted an afternoon television talk show. I believe it was called *The Anne Ramey Program*. Even the subdued nature of the afternoon program was not without mishaps. Once, when an interview was concluding, one of the background flats – the phony wall made to look like a living room – suddenly fell over, crashing onto the floor with a great noise. At that moment I saw how a pro acts under fire. Anne Ramey didn't miss a beat. She cast a quick glance at the fallen flat, turned to the camera and said something to the effect that "a little housekeeping seems to be required."

Besides being Mr. Mike, hanging lights and learning studio camera, I also had another job. CJCH ran an afternoon quiz show called *Domino* sponsored by Dominion Stores. The show was hosted by Bill Ozard. It was a bingo-type program where Ozard stood in front of a board and called out numbers on balls that popped out of a machine. People picked up their cards at Dominion stores and played for prizes. My job was behind the set operating a light board. When Bill called a number I flicked the light switch on and off that corresponded to the number he had mentioned. Bill and I have remained good friends and are still in touch today.

It was during my year at CJCH Television that I worked on my first news program, albeit just as a lowly member of the studio crew but still it was a serious news program and the guest was a man of distinction. Lester B. Pearson was Prime Minister of Canada at the time and he came to the studio one Saturday afternoon to be interviewed by news director Joe King. Of course, this was before the Kennedy assassination and the world was a more relaxed place.

Pearson was driven to the studio in a little grey Austin accompanied by one man. There was no police escort, no contingent of RCMP, no bodyguards, no press secretaries, personal assistant or public relations people. He was not trailed by a bevy of reporters with cameras and microphones. It was Mike Pearson, leader of the Liberal Party, Prime Minister of Canada and winner of the Nobel Peace Prize. He took off his coat and shook hands with all of us. There was no grandeur about him, just a simple, homespun dignity.

He was interviewed for half an hour on subjects ranging from the Cold War to Canadian politics. This was a news special and one of the few local programs videotaped to be played later that evening. Almost everything else was live, including many of our commercials, which brings me to one of my biggest blunders.

Hitting Miss Anne on the head was a mistake you didn't want to repeat, but it didn't cost the station any money. Unfortunately, my next blunder did. It concerned a commercial for Dominion stores. A great deal of produce and foodstuff arrived at the station so viewers could see the weekly specials during these commercials. The products were displayed on a riser consisting of a series of shelves built in our carpentry shop. When the commercial was over, the food was repacked in cartons and taken to the shipping area to be returned to the store. The setting up and taking down of such displays was part of the crew's job.

One day while the rest of the crew lounged in the control room, I passed a commercial set up and incorrectly assumed the commercial had already gone to air. I thought it might show initiative and earn a few badly needed brownie points if I packed up the food, put the cartons on the dolly and took everything back to the shipping area. If I had only bothered to check with the control room. I thought it would be a nice surprise for my colleagues.

In turn, they were waiting for the live break in a CTV network show to do the commercial. You can imagine their consternation and my chagrin when they sauntered out to the studio to discover the shelves were empty, the food was gone and they had no commercial. With less than a minute before the live insert, you discover how fast people can hustle while shouting excitedly and tearing back to alert master control that they had to fill the sixty-second spot with something or other because some airhead had carted away the merchandise.

Despite such frequent goofs I learned a lot about television during my year at CJCH. My original dream was to be a television director but the more I saw of that job the less it appealed to me. I was becoming more attracted to other aspects of the industry. News became of interest to me and so did radio. Radio was uncomplicated compared to television. You didn't need a crew, cameras or lights. But more than anything, radio was highly personal and immediate. I liked the idea of that type of communication but I knew my limitations. I was untrained for such an on-air vocation. I needed more education, training and fine-tuning in the communications industry. Also, the atmosphere in the studio was getting me down. I didn't want to spend more time in the middle of constant bickering between studio crews. There were good men on both crews but the displays of pettiness often bothered me. After a year I was restless, ready for a new environment and a new challenge.

In other words, Mr. Mike looked in the Magic Mirror and saw the bigger world outside.

2

Boston, 1963

Off to Boston

In the spring of 1963, I was accepted into the communications program of the Cambridge School in Boston. I was with students who had graduated from large American high schools that offered such courses as German, Latin and Biology. They'd studied arts and science courses unavailable to me. I'd been out of high school a couple of years and was never much of a student when I attended. But Boston was different. I was suddenly a serious student prepared for the hard work required.

I was assigned a dormitory on Commonwealth Avenue where I could overlook the early construction of the Prudential Center. The building, now part of the Boston skyline, rose floor by floor until it towered above its neighbours. It was significant because as part of its official opening, Perry Como did one of his last big television specials from the new auditorium. I was a reporter for WCSB, the school's student radio station, and I wheedled an invitation to the dress rehearsal. Among Como's guests were Lena Horne and Frankie Lane. Also making a guest appearance was Jayne Mansfield, who at that time was Marilyn Munro's closest rival as the sex goddess of the silver screen. Mansfield died six weeks later in a horrendous car crash, along with her husband Ron Hargitay. Years later, I would play a bit part in a movie with her daughter, Mariska Hargitay of *Law & Order Special Victims Unit* fame. Six weeks after Jack Kennedy stood an arm's length away from me, he was dead too. It was one of those coincidences in life and death that made you think you had bad karma.

John Fitzgerald Kennedy, President of the United States, was a politician in an age when politicians weren't so different than they are today but the press was. Much was swept under the carpet in the 1960s. The press looked the other way. Personal misdemeanours went unreported. Kennedy might be criticized for inept policies or for getting the United States involved in Vietnam but not for more personal dalliances. Personalities have always been easier to cover than policies. Policies may be wrong-headed and ill-conceived but they don't have mistresses, they don't steal, don't drink and drive or try to pick up people in public washrooms. Only their wording and intent display human weaknesses. The fact that policies are longer lasting and control our lives doesn't matter. It is the personality that captures our attention. That was just as true in Kennedy's era as it is today.

Kennedy's death gave us the first real impact of television news and after that TV cameras were poking around Vietnamese villages, bringing home not a war with honour but something far more brutal. The images on the nightly news showed poor people suffering from U.S. bullets and bombs and it had a radical impact on society and the media. Television brought the war home and although newspapers did most of the digging on Watergate, television carried the hearings and the news conferences into our living rooms. Until Richard Nixon, powerful men remained shielded. There were no Monica Lewinskys to show off dress stains.

Vietnam ushered in the era of the probing camera, then ushered in the probing press. As the Pill was liberating women, journalism was also liberated and society would never be the same. My time in Boston coincided with a tumultuous and violent period in the city's history.

I saw Jack Kennedy in September of 1963 soon after arriving in Boston, at a time when only his aides and closest friends knew of his womanizing. My first glimpse of him was in his open limousine as it sped by in a small presidential motorcade of only four motorcycles in advance and a couple of unmarked Secret Service cars. The second time, just a few hours later, was such a strange encounter it still remains a very vivid memory.

Let me set the scene: it was a beautiful autumn Saturday and I'd asked a Canadian girl to go exploring around the city with me. We were close to Beacon Street in the Back Bay area when Kennedy's motorcade first whisked by. There was nothing official and few people were on the street, except those curious as to why police had blocked off the side streets. Already developing my nosy newsman habit, I inquired and a motorcycle cop informed me Kennedy was on his way to a function at the nearby Sheraton Hotel and they wanted the motorcade to proceed unimpeded.

Once Kennedy passed, looking tanned and relaxed, the girl and I decided to wander over to the Sheraton to see if we could get a closer look at him. We did indeed get a better look. The presidential limo was parked by a side door of the hotel and there was virtually no one around. Whatever Kennedy was doing in the hotel didn't take long, for in less than twenty minutes he and his driver exited and got in the limo. As it left the hotel with two motorcycle policemen leading the car, only a dozen people remained on the sidewalk. We stood right at the edge near the road. The limo moved along the hotel driveway travelling at a very slow speed and swung into the street where we stood.

This was in the days before world leaders had a small army of bodyguards. On that autumn afternoon in 1963, Kennedy looked like a man very comfortable with power. The open limo went by us at a crawl and we were so close we could touch him. Then this man, leader of the most powerful nation on earth, did the strangest thing. My date was standing directly in front of me and as Kennedy went by, he gave her what could only be described as a head-to-toe appraisal, scanning her up and down as some guy might do in a bar. I was flabbergasted.

"You've just been given the once-over by the President of the United States," I said but she already knew. It seemed such an odd action for a world leader. Of course, I gained a better understanding after his death when details emerged about his philandering and lustful ways. As Henry Kissinger once said, "Power is a great aphrodisiac."

A few weeks later, Kennedy was dead and the United States mourned as did much of the rest of the world.

By November, I had a part-time job at a small clothing store on Boylston Street. A man entered the store and said, "President Kennedy has been shot in Texas." The store owner sent me to the basement to retrieve an old radio. Once the story was confirmed, the owner promptly closed the store and sent us home. This was perhaps an hour after the shooting but the usually busy downtown Boston was already deserted. Those images of Kennedy on that day six weeks earlier kept replaying in my mind as I walked along the empty streets. I passed a woman who was weeping. The eerie silence was palpable. A great gloom settled over the city. That was the day television changed society and the media.

Jack Kennedy was a much loved president. His youthful charm gave Americans confidence following the rapid consumerism of the 1950s. He gave people the national challenge of putting a man on the moon. It was a lofty goal and it showed leadership. In foreign affairs Kennedy was a disaster. Although he stood up to the Russians over Cuba, he led the United States into the Vietnam War. Thousands of lives and billions of dollars couldn't stave off the ultimate defeat and the beginning of the decline of the United States as a truly great nation. Empires rise and fall but in antiquity their period of domination seemed to go on forever. The imperial British Empire collapsed in a century by making some of the same mistakes. On their spiral downward from such heights the British spent forty years in Iraq.

The United States has never fully recovered from Vietnam but in a society more consumed with style than substance, it is Kennedy's star appeal and image that are remembered. A few decades or a century or two of time will change the perspective on his leadership more than on hero worship.

Boston did not recover quickly from the assassination of its favourite son. The murder of Lee Harvey Oswald a few days later brought an element of undignified bungling to the tragedy. There wasn't much dignified about the prolonged investigation or the often bizarre and ridiculous theories over who and how many actually did the shooting. Remember the grassy knoll? This is a short commentary I wrote on assassination theories. It pretty well sums up my feelings today.

Commentary: September 18, 1978

The United States is turned on to the constant re-examination of its recent history to determine if indeed Americans and the world got the real truth the first time around.

Nowhere is this more evident than in the House of Representatives Assassination Committee with yet another probe digging around for new dirt in the shooting fifteen years ago of President Jack Kennedy. This popular trend is born, raised and fostered by the number of pop writers and charlatans ready to rip off the public by producing books based not on fact but on unconfirmed suspicion and wild-eyed theories. It's as if Americans refuse to believe one sick little man with a good eye and a high-powered rifle shot their president. It is more likely Lee Harvey Oswald had help from Cuban agents in terms of money or encouragement than that he had other gunmen with him that day in Dallas, but even the Cuban connection is not supported by any proof.

Then there is the death of Martin Luther King [Jr.], again with the unproven theory of another gunman. The only person claiming there was a mystery man named Raoul is James Earle Ray, a habitual liar, an admitted rapist, a man of poor character and changing stories.

There might be something positive in these wild theories if there was any new proof to substantiate them, but there isn't anything new. No new documentation, no new witnesses; just more wild unsubstantiated theories. For the buffs of unsupported theories and creative imaginations, the latest investigations, no matter how thorough, would not stop them, and they'll cry foul once more to sell their books based on unsupported allegations and far-out fiction.

The Boston Strangler

When Kennedy was killed, Bostonians already had other problems. The city was reeling from a serial killer, known as the Boston Strangler.

The strangler story hit me right in the face as soon as I arrived in the city. There had just been another murder and the newspapers were outdoing each other. Powerful people might be shielded but murder could lead to a feeding frenzy. What the public didn't know at the time was that some of the details were withheld by police and aided the investigation many months later when authorities started questioning Albert DeSalvo. The Boston tabloid *Record American* was highly critical of the police investigation, and as the murders mounted there was a great deal of frustration and tension in the air. The truth was no one felt safe anymore.

The strangler story started in June of 1962 when an elderly woman named Anna Slesers was found murdered and sexually assaulted in her apartment. The crime was very gruesome even for veteran detectives. Then there was a similar murder on June 30 and another one on July 2. One of the women had been violated with a broomstick. They had all been strangled. The police had no suspects, although there was a certain pattern to the crimes. Thus began one of the strangest and most widespread manhunts in the history of crime. For a student reporter it was an incredible time to be caught up in the public reaction to the horrid events and excitable anticipation.

There was no quick resolution, and the heinous crimes continued through 1963 and into January of 1964. By then fourteen women were dead and the city was in a state of unparalleled panic. Police were under terrible pressure to make an arrest and with every murder that pressure mounted. You could feel the transformation of the city's daily life. In the first years of the murders there had been a certain predictability. The real frenzy came when the pattern and the victims changed. Suddenly it was not just elderly women but also younger victims. No woman was safe and with mounting public pressure, politicians as well as police were taking a beating. People were demanding something be done. By 1964 the city's nerves were raw.

I witnessed firsthand how one man could impose incredible fear on an entire metropolitan area. Fear was in the air, so palpable you could taste it. The lifestyle of the city changed overnight, transforming it into a much more somber place. City life was altered to sterile sidewalks where no woman walked alone. Kennels were sold out of large dogs. Locksmiths worked extra hours. People were afraid and police exasperated. I strolled the streets of the city and one night a police cruiser pulled up and searched my lunch bag. Thousands of lunch bags, book bags and car trunks were opened but still no arrest was forthcoming. As the months dragged by with more murders, the police rounded up the greatest collection of misfits ever corralled in any one city. To complicate matters, people confessed to being the strangler for fame or notoriety or because voices told them to. Weird confessions piled up but out there somewhere the monster remained.

The wrath of the public rained down on the heads of the politicians and they knew something had to be done. The main law enforcement official of Massachusetts was the state's Attorney General, Edward Brooke. He announced the establishment of a Strangler Bureau. This coordinated force would devote all of its time and energies to the capture and conviction of the Boston Strangler. Brooke appointed lawyer John Bottomly as the bureau's coordinator. It was a strange appointment as Bottomly's background was in real estate, not criminal apprehension. The governor then announced a reward of $10,000 for information leading to an arrest.

During the next six months over a thousand tips were received. Some were honest attempts to help and some were from people out of touch with reality. Investigators fanned out in all directions and hauled in a host of unsavoury characters. They ranged from mildly maladjusted to dreadfully ill people with kinky perversions and outrageous habits. In the offices of the Strangler Bureau, a large board faced against the wall to conceal the photos of the victims. Their number was growing – eight, nine, ten, eleven, twelve ... Some were young, some were old, some lived in the city, some in the suburbs. Some may have been killed by the strangler while others may have been murdered by other people. I followed the story while working for WCSB, the school radio station. It was the last murder that brought the grizzly crimes close in a rather personal way.

The victim was nineteen-year-old Mary Sullivan, who lived at 44A Charles Street, directly across from a small coffee house called Sheriff's. It was a place my friends and I used to frequent when there was time to socialize. Mary Sullivan's nude body was discovered by her two roommates in early January 1964. A crowd gathered outside her apartment building to try to view the macabre scene. She had been strangled. The body looked as if it had been deliberately positioned on the bed, legs splayed with a Christmas card by her foot that said Seasons Greetings. It brought the strangler to my neighbourhood.

When the strangler was finally captured in November 1965, a great relief swept over the city but it was also anticlimactic. When he confessed, providing details only the police knew, Albert DeSalvo was already in custody in a mental hospital. What was so outrageous about the long and fruitless investigation was the fact DeSalvo had a lengthy police record. He was known as both the Measuring Man and the Green Man, depending on which part of New England you were living in. In Connecticut DeSalvo would pass himself off as an agent for a modelling agency. They were looking for models of all shapes and sizes, he said, and unsuspecting women let him into their homes as he required a form to be completed and, oh yes, did he mention he had to take down their measurements? There were no assaults or violence. He simply took the women's measurements and left. Because of the lack of violence, the authorities explained, DeSalvo's criminal profile slipped beneath their radar. They were looking for violent offenders. As unbelievable as it sounds, that's truly what happened.

It should be noted that today there are different theories about the Boston Strangler. People who spent years studying the cases do not believe Albert DeSalvo committed all the murders. In 2001, through modern forensics and exhuming his body, it was proven he didn't in fact kill Mary Jane Sullivan. There have been many books written about the Boston Strangler. One of the best is Susan Kelley's *The Boston Strangler*, which I think has a more realistic look at the murders. Certainly Albert DeSalvo knew things about some of the killings that only the murderer could know. Because he was already institutionalized, he was never charged with the crimes and ultimately was stabbed to death while incarcerated. How many of the women he really killed will never be known. Above all, what remains with me was the remarkable fear imposed on the entire large metropolitan area and the inability of authorities to do anything about it.

The Boston Mob or Never Carry Your Gun in a Paper Bag When One of Your Hands has Been Blown Off

Dramatic as it was, the strangler wasn't the only man making city streets unsafe. A vicious gang war was also underway that ultimately produced far more bodies than the strangler. The feud was between the Irish Charlestown mob run by the McLaughlin Brothers and a mob from Summerville headed by James Buddy McLean. The feud was not so much about vying for jurisdiction as the settling of an old score, and the cast of characters read like something out of a pulp fiction magazine.

It started at a Labor Day picnic when Punchy McLaughlin's brother tried to grope the girlfriend of a fellow mobster. Punchy's brother was beaten senseless and the McLaughlin brothers sought revenge. Bodies started piling up on both sides. These men were not criminal masterminds but small-time hoods, the musclemen for loan sharks – those people who broke your kneecap if you didn't pay your debts. There was a great deal of money involved in loan sharking. Millions of dollars a week was the take for the big boys and they hired the most violent, vicious men to collect their money. The more despicable the reputation, the more you were ensured payment.

One of the more grizzly murders I remember was a decapitated body behind the steering wheel with the head in the trunk. There was a cynical perspective to this mayhem. The police were busy with the strangler and if another gangster was eliminated – well, so much the better. That was the public attitude as well. It was gangsters wiping out other gangsters. Not a big deal for that matter, and good riddance. Except, of course, violence always spills over to the innocent. A young man, a student, either got in the way or was mistaken for someone else. He was shot to death and the public, with their pent-up emotions, responded in a fury.

Let me tell you a personal story to illustrate how tense things were. I went into a Chinese restaurant one night to order takeout. Once I placed my order, I waited on a small settee. Booths lined the wall opposite. The place was empty except for one elderly Chinese gentleman, sitting directly across from me in one of the booths. Even the lady who took my order had disappeared into the kitchen. I had one of those moments we all experience, when the thought occurs that you may not have brought your wallet. I quickly reached into the inside pocket of my sport coat just as my eyes made contact with the elderly gentleman. When he saw my hand dive into my pocket, he dropped his eating utensils and put his hands in the air. It was one of those quintessential moments where time stands still. Did he think I was going to shoot him? Did I look like a hit man, a hoodlum? Was he just hallucinating or expecting to be murdered? We sat frozen like images in a photograph. Without taking my eyes off him, I slowly removed my wallet. He lowered his arms and looked at his food. It was just another small encounter in a city filled with tension.

A Mink, a Cloth Coat and a Close Call

My head was spinning with the violent, vicious happenings swirling around me. I had a regular shift in the school radio station, spinning records and preparing newscasts. The news was filled with the stories of the street. I was also working part-time at Morton's Incorporated, the biggest ladies store in New England. Many readers may be familiar with Morton's. It was located at 89 Causeway Street, across from North Station, where the Boston Bruins used to play. It was a big store with three large floors of apparel in what was called "the finest quality fashions for ladies and girls."

My job was in the suit and coat department on the second floor. I was the stock boy for the floor but in fact I did everything. I learned a lot about the fashion world and its quick rejection of last year's rave review. What was "hot" one season was definitely not the next. The buyer for our department was Mr. Hassler, who was often in New York, looking for that next "hot" item that would sell fast so there wasn't a lot of stock around when the season was over. There was keen competition among the store's buyers and the mark of their success was how much stock remained at the end of season. A rack of unsold items was an indictment.

My first season at Morton's the buyer purchased several hundred cashmere knee-length coats with fox collars. They were our big sellers in early autumn and sold for the princely sum of $119. They sold well the first months with fifty percent of the garments scooped up by customers. The store had made its profit by then. The next twenty-five percent of the stock sold throughout the winter at a reduced price of $89. In March they were further reduced to $69 then to $49. A year later the remaining dozen coats were on the bargain rack for $19.95. Fashion is quirky and nothing depreciates like last year's style, whether it is a car or a coat.

There were five sales ladies on the floor, endearing women who had worked in the store for years. I don't remember all their names but I do recall Mrs. Reardon and Mrs. Kaufman.

Mrs. Reardon was a big, red-haired Irish woman and Mrs. Kaufman, a petit Jewish lady with thick glasses that made her eyes look particularly pleading. When there were no customers on the floor, the ladies had their own chairs, each placed strategically in front of a changing room. They would talk among themselves about grandchildren, children and the affairs in their families and Boston politics. They were the picture of everybody's grandmother and sold a lot of apparel with their kindly approach. They also worked hard, putting in a six-day workweek with long hours, much of which they stood on their feet. They were competitive too, haggling over commissions. Every few months a major flare-up among the sales women had Mr. Hassler intervene. Once Mrs. Reardon spit in Mrs. Kaufman's face and there was a great donnybrook with hair-pulling, pushing and, of course, the inevitable weepy aftermath. Then customers suddenly appeared on the floor and sweetness quickly resumed. The ladies were professional. They knew why they were there. Nothing stood in the way of selling. Personal feelings could be dealt with later.

I loved working at Morton's. The assistant buyer was Harvey Goldman, a young man not much older than I was. Except for singers Ian and Sylvia he didn't know much about Canada but he was a genial guy and we got along. Harvey was heading into a career in fashion. I wasn't, but I liked the variety of the work. When there were many customers I could be found behind the counter folding newly purchased items in tissue and putting them into the fancy boxes that had "Morton's" embossed on the side.

One Saturday afternoon we were unusually busy. Even Mr. Hassler was on the floor selling and he only did that when all the sales ladies were serving customers. I was assisting on the counter, boxing coats, sweaters, suits and slacks. I was courteous and I worked fast. We had one of those pneumatic vacuum systems where the cash was put in a tube and shot up to the third floor. A minute later the receipt and change shot back to our counter. The system kept all the cash and accounting in a central location, which was convenient but in extremely busy times the system was just slow enough to back up the customers waiting for their change and receipts.

It was at such a time that one of the grandmothers sold the most expensive coat on the floor, a short mink jacket of very high quality. I wrapped it up and then wrapped one of the $19.95 specials – the last of the cashmeres with the fox collars. We didn't know about the mix-up until the lady who had purchased the mink stopped to show off her new jacket to one of her friends. Imagine the consternation when she opened the box and found a $19 cloth coat where her mink should have been. When she flew back to our counter we all realized my mistake.

"Find the customer with the mink," Mr. Hassler snapped. "She may still be in the store."

Filled with trepidation and the prospect of losing my job I raced through the crowd. If the woman was gone would I have to pay back the store's loss? Would I lose my job? Would I be hauled up before the president of the company? I wasn't even certain what the woman looked like. I scanned the customers coming and going. I was looking for a needle in a haystack. Then I saw her just as she was going out the door. As she was about to step onto the sidewalk, I took her arm and said, "Excuse me, madam, but I think I gave you the wrong item." I brought her back to the counter on the second floor, where her eyes widened when I opened the box and, sure enough, there was the missing mink.

"A close one," the buyer said and we all agreed. A very close one.

By the time I graduated from Cambridge, the gangland feud was still going on. The loan sharks and their enforcers were still blasting away at each other and the carnage was mounting. Forty-three people had died. Research shows less than half a dozen of the murders were ever solved. If there was justice it was the rough justice meted out on the street. After several attempts on his life Punchy McLaughlin was shot to death getting on a bus in the Roxbury section of the city. His gun was concealed in a paper bag and since one of his hands had already been shot off in a previous attempt on his life, he couldn't defend himself quickly enough.

As for me I was offered a job as an announcer in St. Johnsbury, Vermont, which I would have eagerly accepted except my student visa was expiring and I wasn't a U.S. citizen.

Under the rules of the Federal Communications Commission, I couldn't turn on the transmitters or operate the equipment and in a small station you did everything. So I came back to Canada for a less hectic existence.

3

Newcastle, 1965–1966

The Community Voice of the Miramichi

After the turmoil in Boston, returning to Nova Scotia was like entering a world of tranquility. Hitchhiking from town to town I tramped up the stairs of one small radio station after another: Bridgewater, Kentville, New Glasgow and Antigonish, sitting in unfamiliar radio announcer booths, auditioning for on-air jobs when there weren't any openings. Managers usually gave me an audition because they never knew for sure and staff changes can happen quickly.

Even the urgent need for a job didn't reduce the peacefulness I felt. I was seeing Nova Scotia through new eyes, walking the roads and it was evident times were changing. The Stanfield government had established Industrial Estates Ltd. and new industry was growing everywhere. Something else was evident too. I no longer took for granted the natural beauty that had surrounded me most of my life. Even so, if there was no job in Nova Scotia I would move on. I borrowed a friend's tape recorder and sent audition tapes far and wide, reading stories out of newspapers. These tapes were pretty crude but after a few weeks of trying I finally secured a position as a staff announcer at New Brunswick radio station CKMR in Newcastle, 790 on your radio dial, "The Community Voice of the Miramichi."

CKMR

What a cornucopia of work it was. I hosted programs spinning records, giving the weather, reading commercials, preparing newscasts and occasionally conducting interviews. CKMR was a traditional small-town radio station in the 1960s when rock 'n' roll was at its vanguard and the hit parade tunes of the day are now considered golden oldies. It wasn't just rock we played. There was a daily dose of country music, Sunday morning hymns and church services, plus Frank Sinatra and Percy Faith.

The station was above a Western Tire store with ten people on staff and a few part-timers. This was in the era before women broke the barrier of broadcasting and radio remained a male domain. The only woman on staff full-time was the receptionist. Half the employees were young announcers, getting their feet wet in commercial radio and eager to move on to bigger markets.

I was assigned the midday shift where I hosted a multitude of programs, all with different types of music. Someone who loved alliteration had given the programs their titles. *Turntable Terrace*, *Tea Time Tunes*, *Hayshakers Hoedown* – whoopee! Titles have a curious significance along the Miramichi River. Newcastle was nestled along its banks and had a small tree-lined square in its centre. The neighbouring town of Chatham was on the other side of the river. When I lived there the towns hadn't yet adopted the grandiose, overblown name of Miramichi City.

Death by Funeral Announcement

The radio station had one feature that brought fear into the hearts of all the young announcers. Sponsors were allowed to write their own commercials. If they were well paying sponsors they could even fudge (or totally disregard) the time limit on a commercial. Some one-minute commercials were seventy seconds or longer. When you were on the air live, trying to get through single-spaced copy that defied articulation, such commercials lasted a lifetime.

The scariest of them all was the copy for the Stoddard Mercantile, a general purpose hardware store where the proprietor not only wrote his own commercials but listened keenly to make sure his work of art was read properly. For young announcers a Stoddard Mercantile commercial was an on-air disaster waiting to happen. It contained wordy jawbreakers, compound sentences, little or no punctuation and price lists without commas. Lost in the middle of the copy, you never knew exactly where to start and stop. Rewriting was out of the question. We weren't allowed to change a word. Coming on shift, announcers looked through the program log to see what commercials we faced. One Stoddard Mercantile was bad, two were horrible and three were a catastrophe.

But problematic as some of the commercials were, the funeral announcements were worse. Newcastle did some very quirky things with proper names and the English language in general. Linguists came from afar to study this area that retained some of the oldest English words and pronunciations in existence. These included proper nouns and family names. Then there were the family feuds that split households into separate camps, driving brothers and sisters so far apart they used different pronunciations for the same name. One was the name Mahoney. It was pronounced Ma-*hon*-ney with the emphasis on the second syllable by one branch of the family and *Ma*-hawn-knee with the emphasis on the first syllable by another branch.

The funeral directors wrote their own announcements and sometimes they included the family pronunciation and sometimes they didn't. At times we would call the funeral parlour to double-check, but often didn't have a chance and got it wrong on the air. If we announced, "The late Mr. Fred Ma*hon*ey was resting at So and So's funeral home with services scheduled for Friday," and dear God in Heaven, it wasn't right, wasn't Mrs. *Ma*-hawn-knee on the phone giving us a good piece of her mind for being such knuckleheads. We played organ music behind these announcements and sounded very solemn. We were. Funeral announcements were serious business. You might suspect young announcers would try to tie each other up during such presentations but one good reprimand carried ominous memories. I've been eternally grateful that once I left Newcastle I never had to read another funeral announcement. And may all who struggled through seventy seconds of the Stoddard Mercantile, now rest in peace.

The CBC

CKMR was a CBC affiliate. Every couple of hours we would switch to the network for a national program or the news from Toronto. One of the CBC announcers with a smooth and flawless delivery was a guy named Alex Trebek, who left the corporation to go Stateside and become famous as host of Jeopardy.

These were the 1960s and the old golden days of CBC Radio when its broadcasts were more directed at specific audiences and chock full of practical information. *The Fisheries Broadcast and Farm Report*, *Neighbourly News* and *Maritime Gardener* were all useful information. It wasn't trying to probe the depth of Mrs. Jones's psyche or be as funky and hip as it tries to be today.

At least CBC Radio is Canadian in content. CBC Television is another matter.

It is discouraging to see all efforts to overhaul CBC Television fall so far short of the mark. The manner in which the CBC covers outside criticism of itself shows how thin-skinned the corporation can be. With their own closets full of skeletons, CTV and Global aren't interested in expanding any story that might involve lack of Canadian content, so we have the same scenario playing over and over. If someone criticizes the CBC or suggests a more enlightened policy for public broadcasting, the CBC quickly dusts off someone like Ian Morrison and his Friends of Canadian Broadcasting, who offer a ten-second rebuttal and the story withers and dies even if the criticism is valid. That's how the CBC covers criticism of public broadcasting. There are the occasional public inquiries and some produce excellent recommendations. Others miss the boat completely. It hardly matters if they're not acted upon. Here's a commentary I wrote years after CKMR, following the 1996 probe into public broadcasting.

Commentary: Why Not a Different CBC?

Following the trials and tribulations of the CBC through the landscape of Canadian politics and public interest is a bit like following a path that doesn't have a final destination.

There is yet another indeterminable report on the future of the CBC – this one conducted by three people who, it seems to me, didn't follow the mandate given them to find a unique form for public broadcasting. Instead they've found a new tax, left many of the inefficiencies untouched and failed to find a new CBC. The report is not without merit. Pierre Juneau, Peter Herrndorf and Catherine Murray do recommend scrapping U.S. programming, finally making the CBC what it should have been years ago – Canadian. This is positive as are some other things.

But the report contains glaring inconsistencies. Doing away with most sports but keeping some sports – half in sports, half out of sports and as usual, trying to be all things to all people.

I thought the point and purpose of this study was to produce a path for public broadcasting into the next century. I believe in public broadcasting; it's good for Canada. It's even good for private broadcasting because it keeps standards higher and competition keener. But I don't get this. Where's the map, where's the future, where's the final destination? This report tries to define public broadcasting but it gives us a big taste of the status quo. It leaves a cash-starved infrastructure in place, fails to effectively deal with an overblown bureaucracy and lets the CBC become an increasingly irrelevant service and, of course, puts another tax on Canadians.

It isn't good enough because it isn't enough. Back to the drawing board as that path keeps getting longer.

* * *

Of course, the best of the recommendations were never acted upon and our public broadcaster still runs U.S. programming as if it weren't a public broadcaster at all. But it is, and it should stop acting like CTV.

Airwaves Ownership

It isn't mentioned much anymore but the airwaves still belong to the people of Canada. The question is how well Canadians are served for the money spent. Are we showcasing enough Canadian films and documentaries? Almost all filmmakers and documentary producers will say no. Are we highlighting enough Canadian actors? Most actors would say no. Are we providing enough work for our writers? Most writers would say no and so would set designers, producers, lighting technicians, carpenters and painters. If we aren't reflecting our history, our arts and artists then we aren't reflecting Canada.

CBC television looks as slick as the private networks but being slick isn't terribly important. PBS in the United States isn't slick but it is very effective. When the lead program for the CBC's 6 p.m. news program is a U.S. sitcom, that doesn't show much of a commitment to Canadian content. CBC executives always defend the corporation without acknowledging they really want a large audience. Let the privates chase the ratings. Canadian content and Canadian artists suffer because the CBC wants numbers. Its priorities are skewed and the artistic community pays for that mistake. This contention is based on one unassailable fact. The more programs we make, the better they will be. The Canadian production industry has already demonstrated it can do great work. Why isn't it doing more of it?

The Privates

The amount of Canadian content carried by our private television networks is totally disgraceful. Also lamentable is the fact the once strong CRTC now seems to be a toothless tiger that has let the giant corporations pour out their weepy tale of immense challenges and exorbitant costs so they are permitted to run cheaper U.S. programs and make billions in profits. It's even more cause for alarm when corporations such as Bell and CanWest buy up more of the market with the very profits they should be spending on Canadian content. We have permitted such corporations to dilute our culture for the almighty dollar. There is no good reason why CBC is not totally Canadian. Nor is there an excuse for private networks not to be sixty to seventy percent Canadian during prime time. More made-in-Canada programming means more jobs and money in the hands of thousands of people circulating through the economy. That's better than having it circulate through the boardrooms of Global and CTV and their parent companies, which is currently the case.

End of rant.

Moving on to Moncton

"This is 790 on your radio dial, CKMR – the community voice of the Miramichi." That was the station ID, then there would be a CBC station break and Alex Trebek would come on with the national news. I took off my headphones and walked across the small lobby to the closet where the teletype machine was spewing out the latest news summary from the Canadian Press, looking for any local New Brunswick or Maritime stories I could also use. I was on the air in five minutes so it was rip and read with no time for rewrites. CKMR was bare-bones broadcasting but I was making $50 a week, getting lots of air time and honing my skills.

After fifteen months I was certain I wanted to move into the news business. I sent audition tapes to Maritime stations and one paid off. I landed my first full-time news job in Moncton and news would consume me for the next thirty-four years.

4

Moncton, 1967

Driving my Newscast Across Town

A few months later I was trying to see the road through the white blur of a raging snowstorm. My hands gripped the wheel as the wind drove the snow directly at me. By that time I had been ensconced in radio news, working the night shift at CKCW in Moncton. But this night I was to make my very first appearance on television. My newscast was on the seat beside me, a silent passenger experiencing the harrowing adventure of a blizzard. Was there, I wondered, anything in the code of journalism etched on a wall somewhere, similar to the mail carrier's pledge, through wind and snow and hail?

I was the only newsman I knew who took his newscast for a drive. Certainly the information on the passenger's seat that I had carefully crafted back in the radio newsroom contained nothing as exciting as what I was experiencing at that moment. There were no cars on the streets. Who would be out in this weather? Just me and my newscast travelling across Moncton at such a late hour to serve only New Brunswick's severest insomniacs.

CKCW was a much different station than Newcastle. Moncton had a regular newsroom, not a closet with a teletype. But the radio and television operations were not only in separate buildings, but in separate parts of the city.

Most young broadcasters would be nervous at the prospect of their premier television appearance. Getting to the station was far more nerve-wracking than actually being on air. I had been in news long enough to have covered my first city council, experienced my first municipal budget and filed my first national report. I was still green but not as green as when I arrived.

First Assignment

It is still my first story that stands out the strongest. Nothing quite compared to the weeping couple entwined in each other's arms, watching their house being engulfed in flames. Maybe that night it was my understanding too of what lay ahead in my chosen vocation. I would constantly be broaching sensitive areas as I was then, the second day on the job. It was the deadline too, always there would be a deadline. Ninety minutes before the major radio newscast and I was so green and unfamiliar with Moncton, one of the technicians offered to drive me to the scene because the rookie had to get the story and get back fast.

The stark images of that early winter evening have certainly stayed with me much longer than I would have imagined. Things fade over time, the memory plays tricks, but I can still remember the deadening daylight on the western horizon and the wind-whipped flames with a searing angry edge that hissed as they licked the wet ground. With no chance of saving the house, the efforts of the firemen were containment, to keep the blaze from spreading. What the owners possessed remained inside and lost forever.

I was reluctant to approach them at such an intimate moment. Silhouetted in the orange glow they looked frail and defeated. Fires are usually scenes of lament. Victims belong there, as do tears, firemen, hoses and axes and yes, even spectators. They are a natural part of the landscape. I was the only intruder closing in on the weeping couple. At close range every detail of their anguish was reflected by the flames.

My questions were rudimentary. The wife did the talking, her curt answers coming in short gasps. Their name was LeBlanc. Yes, they owned the house and no, they didn't have any insurance. It was difficult to hear her over the firemen and the torrents of water slowly, very slowly, defeating the still stubborn flames. Husband and wife stood bewildered by the reporter with his open notebook. The three of us formed an island on the front yard. We were too close to the fire really, but no one told us to move. I was with them but I wasn't part of them. It was their misery and I was the intruder, the onlooker. I told them I was sorry for their loss and it sounded ineffectual and weak. I wasn't trained in the protocol of personal detachment. I wasn't a mike boom operator on Romper Room or a student in Boston or a staff announcer in Newcastle. I was doing a different sort of work. I was a newsman.

In future years the revelations of that night would recur. I would often be in sensitive areas, asking questions of people who didn't necessarily want to give me answers. People so bewildered by heartache there were no answers. It is not always a respectable job. I could not wait. I had a deadline. Does it matter if the news gets on the air an hour sooner or later? Today I would say it matters not at all. It's better to get it right than get it first. But in 1967 as a young reporter on my first assignment it mattered a great deal and I didn't want to hear the story secondhand by phoning the police or the fire department later on. I already understood things are often inaccurate.

Police as Reporters

Young reporters I see on television today don't ask as many questions or probe as much due to the profusion of media handlers. This is particularly noticeable in police stories. Reporters often let the police tell much of the story and police departments now have people trained in media-speak to make sure the department is painted in a good light, even when it's messed up an investigation. It's the policemen telling the story, not the reporter.

Reporting by police officer is fast and easy and that's all television news usually requires. The downside of this practice is obvious. It lets the police have too much control over the flow of information. Police don't let reporters make arrests and reporters shouldn't let police tell the story. Good reporters are skeptics who never take the word of anybody in authority. That includes police, the armed forces, public relations flacks and politicians. I'm not saying these people are dishonest. It's just that they have a vested interest in putting their own spin on a story. The first and foremost rule should be – find out for yourself.

The World of 1967

Reporting teaches you a little about a lot of things. In 1967, even to the uninitiated, the world seemed to be spinning faster on its axis. It was the year when hatred and rigidity boiled over in the Middle East in the short and bloody Six Day War. The United States was mired in its own war. Culture and music were shifting under our feet. Young people were breaking away from traditional values. Flower Power and Love-ins shared the news with Vietnam massacres. Dissention was everywhere. Barbara Streisand sang in Central Park to 135,000 people. Three times that number marched down Fifth Avenue in New York in support of U.S. fighting men. When it came to protest, they were in the minority. Massive marches and demonstrations dotted the urban landscape. Mohammad Ali was indicted in Houston for refusing to be one of those fighting men. At the United Nations, President Charles de Gaulle criticized the United States for its role in Southeast Asia. Then he flew into Canada and called for a free Quebec with his famous "Vive Quebec Libre" speech before going off to Paris, leaving the Pearson government in a flap, giving the Separatists a boost and putting a new strain on Anglo-Franco relations that was felt all the way to Moncton.

Aside from de Gaulle, Expo 67 topped Canadian news. Queen Elizabeth and Prince Philip opened Expo and toured parts of the country while another Elizabeth – Taylor – won the Academy Award for *Who's Afraid of Virginia Woolf?*. The edgy movie fit the unsettled times.

With Expo on the world stage Canada had supposedly come of age. The country's future was bright. We were on the cusp of well-being and advancement. We were catching up with Wilfred

Laurier's prediction, "The Twentieth Century Belongs to Canada." We expected not only prosperity but an improved, more efficient and enlightened leadership. No one in 1967 would have believed that forty years later so many of our children would be living in poverty, so many of our students would be dropping out of school and we still haven't got around to reforming or abolishing our senate.

Along with co-host Vince Gallant, who in many respects was my mentor in the news business, we reported on these events five nights a week in a series of radio newscasts, including a complete half-hour summary of local, Canadian and world events at 10 p.m.

The News Cycle

News is cyclical in nature. In fact, the word "news" is actually a non sequitur. There is hardly anything that is new except circumstances. If only truly new news were reported – something that has absolutely never happened before – newspapers would be less than a page and television newscasts would be no more than a minute. There is nothing new about murder, war or corruption except the circumstances. The Six O'clock News would be more accurately called "The Six O'clock Circumstances." To be a little more philosophical, even the circumstances are often similar. Study the many comparisons in substance and style between two wars where the United States got involved due to incredible miscalculations in foreign policy – Iraq and Vietnam. In 2007, arguments for and against the Iraqi war sound strikingly similar to positions and comments on Vietnam in 1967. Governments rise and governments fall. People are caught cheating and stealing over and over again. Only the circumstances change.

After ten years you begin to see the reality of the news cycle. The same stories start to come around again. They have different faces and different locations but the basic facts are the same. When I first covered Halifax City Hall in the 1960s, all the talk was about the Cogswell Street interchange and the cat problem. They were talking of building the interchange then, now they're talking of tearing it down. As for cats? Well, they're still at the talking stage.

Leonard Jones

Leonard Jones was the controversial mayor of Moncton in 1967. He came to national attention a few years later when Robert Stanfield refused to sign his nomination papers as a Progressive Conservative candidate in the federal election. Many in the Conservative Party were worried Jones was anti-French and would be labelled a racist when the Conservatives needed inroads in Quebec.

In many respects Jones was a competent mayor but he had a quirky streak. He could blurt out the strangest comments that were sometimes so right wing, it's little wonder the national PC party didn't want him, even if local constituents did. Once a prominent dignitary came to town – I believe it was Jacques Hébert, Pierre Trudeau's great friend. Hébert wore his hair long in the fashionable Beatle cut. When Hébert was taken on a courtesy call to meet the mayor, Jones told him he didn't trust a man whose ears he couldn't see. Hébert stormed out of the mayor's office and the meeting was over.

Needless to say, such a mayor didn't avoid controversy. Leonard Jones spoke his mind on everything, including his rather negative position on extending rights to New Brunswick Acadians. A few years later, students from the French-speaking Université de Moncton put a dead pig on Jones's doorstep.

Full Circle

In subsequent years, Moncton has undergone the most significant transformation of any community in the Maritimes. It lost the CN shops and gained an entirely new upbeat economy. I wasn't there to watch the transformation. In 1968 I received an offer from CJCH to join the Halifax radio newsroom. I had left Halifax six years earlier for training in Boston and practical experience in Newcastle and Moncton. Now I was completing the full circle back to Halifax. It wouldn't be the last circle either.

5

Halifax, 1968

Rock 'n' Roll

I arrived at CJCH Radio at the height of the rock 'n' roll era and CJ, as we called it, was a-rockin. Unlike Moncton with its traditional programming and long newscasts, CJ was rock, all fast and all lively. Gone were the half-hour radio newscasts. At CJ our major newscast at seven and eight in the morning and six in the evening covered ten minutes, including sports and weather. Everything else was five minutes or under. In Moncton, news was always on the hour and the delivery rather slow and deliberate. In Halifax, the news was at five minutes to the hour with a fast, punchy delivery.

In Moncton, you didn't hear the words "competition" or "ratings" or such terms as "number one in the market." In Halifax, those were the buzzwords, the really important things. We were in keen competition with CHNS and the two stations ran neck and neck in news scoops and music scoops too. Getting the new tunes on the air first was a very big deal. If CJ had the latest British hit from the Beatles before CHNS, we played that forty-five over and over, hammering the fact we had the best music and we had it first. CHNS did the same. The Beatles, Elvis – we had all the hits and brother, we played them.

Of course, the competition could always tape our new song right off the air as soon as we played it. To combat such thievery CJ produced a special tape recording that declared in a whispering voice in the middle of a new Beatles record – "A CJCH Exclusive." CHNS did something similar because they too suspected that piracy was a two-way street. Music, particularly new rock music from Britain, was hot property in the 1960s and so was the news.

Coverage

The CJ Radio newsroom covered metro Halifax-Dartmouth like a blanket. We had a dozen staff members, including commentator Edmund Morris. Besides our on-air shifts, we had reporting beats. Dick Prat was the regular Halifax City Hall reporter and when the news overflowed during those tumultuous times, we backed him up.

There was high drama and frayed tempers in Halifax in the late '60s. The world was shifting under our feet. The status quo of past decades was wearing away. At one point, Halifax City Council tried to hire a new city manager from Oklahoma. Word came that the chosen man was anti-union and anti-black. In Halifax, the unions and the blacks already endured enough and people took to the streets. It was the talk of the town and a big story in the news.

At CJ Radio Harris Sullivan was sent to Oklahoma City to interview the controversial figure and investigate his background. To send a radio reporter thousands of miles to chase a local story gives you some idea of our level of competitiveness and the degree of interest in the community. In fact, hostility over the hiring was reaching the boiling point. Race riots were taking place in major U.S. cities and some of that frantic fever made its way north.

The night of the vote on the question of hiring the Oklahoma City manager, Halifax City Council chambers were so crowded, there was standing room only and people became angry and boisterous. Jimmy Bell, the long-time head of the Marine Workers Union, got a rousing ovation when he shouted that people should stop paying taxes. "Damn this city anyway, damn it to hell," someone muttered. There were threats, sneers and plenty of intimidation. The room was hot, anger flared, some people smelled of booze. It was chain lightning ready to flash. I elbowed my way through the crowd to file a quick report back at the station, making my way next door to the alderman's lounge. When I opened the door, I found the room also filled with wall-to-wall police officers – just in case the hostility turned to mayhem. It didn't, because Council wisely voted against hiring the man from Oklahoma. The story was over but the cause of the hostility was not.

It was the 1960s and the poor and disenfranchised were tired of their role in the world. The youth were cynical and our traditional social fabric was ripping before our eyes – rock 'n' roll, changing attitudes and changing social values. Young people were smoking pot, new dances were the rage and new fashions too. It was more than a change – it was a social upheaval.

As the ghettos in American cities burned with looters shown on television taking what they wanted, things got tense in Halifax. The question of race riots was no longer an abstract subject. The Black Panthers came to town. It was only the moderation and good sense of some of the older leaders in the black community – men and women of principle who were respected and listened to – that kept things relatively calm. Although there were some small flare-ups, there was none of the widespread violence we saw on the nightly news in the United States.

Africville

There was lingering anger over Africville too. Moving the small black community didn't create strife among most Nova Scotians, but it certainly did among the people being relocated.

There has been much written about Africville over the years, some of it accurate and some of it exaggerated nonsense. Those who describe Africville as a picturesque, idyllic community nestled on the shores of Bedford Basin are trying to rewrite history and deceive future generations. Few places in Canada have been as falsely depicted as Africville.

What is seldom written in today's pop culture is an accurate description of the cluster of dilapidated houses sitting next to a sprawling city dump. The community was overshadowed with growing mountains of garbage, put there by the city, creating a rat infestation. Africville was unsanitary and settled, in some cases, by squatters. The squatters are seldom mentioned today because that's not how Africville descendants and some magazine writers want to depict it. It makes a better story to point fingers at an uncaring racist city that just wanted to destroy people's homes to make way for a new bridge across Halifax harbour.

There is no denying racism existed all around Africville. The fact that city services were not extended there and a dump allowed to overwhelm the settlement speaks for itself. More than the seagulls atop the mountain of garbage looked down on Africville. Racism had settled over Africville like the thin veil of morning mist, but it had very little to do with the decision to dismantle the community. The procedure was clumsy as city hall initiatives often are. It is unlikely poor white folks would have their belongings hauled away in city dump trucks instead of moving vans.

However, there is more to the story than insensitivity. The deteriorated state of the housing in Africville, the rat problem, the unsanitary conditions and the health risks prompted even social workers who cared deeply about the people of Africville to concede that relocation was the right thing to do.

In addition, the city's mayor at the time was Allen O'Brien, an intellectual with a highly developed social conscience. He should be the last person accused of not caring about people. In most cases the city matched the loss of poor housing with brand new accommodations and compensation. Even the squatters got compensation for losing houses they didn't own. But the smear of racism hangs over Africville. Propaganda and misinformation can drive history as they are turning Africville into a drastically different community. Those who witnessed the real story know the truth but few of them are talking.

I acknowledge that moving people from their homes is poor policy. Just look at relocation programs in northern Canada where the results have been devastating. I also acknowledge we have racists and rascals on both side of the colour barrier ready to exploit any situation.

Naming a Bridge

The official reason for relocating Africville was the construction of the A. Murray MacKay Bridge and the name of the bridge is a story in itself. At the time the bridge was under construction, the Bridge Commission had to come up with a name for the structure. They wanted to call it the Robert L. Stanfield Bridge but Bob said he didn't want a bridge named after him. He wouldn't want an airport either, but when you're dead what can you do?

When Stanfield turned down the offer, the Bridge Commission looked around. They were getting a little frantic. They had to have the name of some distinguished citizen, but apparently distinguished citizens are few and far between and those approached declined the offer. Which only goes to show it's easier to pick the name of someone who can't say no. The Joseph Howe Bridge, for example. But the Bridge Commission didn't go for Joe. They picked one of their own. The bridge would be named after the past chairman of the Bridge Commission, A. Murray MacKay. People were incredulous. A. Murray Who? Most Haligonians, to say nothing of Nova Scotians, had never heard of him.

At CJCH we mounted a vigorous campaign against the Bridge Commission's cronyism. Edmund Morris did a number of commentaries, we went to the streets for people's reaction and some of it was very funny. Suddenly the Bridge Commission came under fire from all quarters. They countered with a sputtering public relations campaign that pictured MacKay as an early pioneer of Nova Scotia's telephone system. If you were naming the bridge after a telephone pioneer, wouldn't Alexander Graham Bell fit the bill? Once members of the Bridge Commission had egg on their faces they refused to wash it off. They stood their ground and the public controversy, driven in large part by our newsroom, finally fizzled. Now A. Murray MacKay is a household name, not because of pioneering the telephone company but because he has a bridge named after him. I still call it the Narrows Bridge, which is probably what the Bridge Commission should have called it in the first place.

Sydney Steel

All the major stories of the '60s in Nova Scotia didn't just happen in Halifax. The closure of Sydney Steel was bigger than the name of a Halifax bridge. When Britain's Hawker-Siddley announced it was closing the mill, thousands of protesters poured into the streets and captured the attention of the nation. Hawker-Siddley gave the pink slip to Cape Breton steelworkers in the late '60s. Robert Stanfield had already left Nova Scotia for the federal stage and his long-time running mate, George Isaac Smith from Truro, was the new premier.

Upon taking office, Smith faced two immediate problems – a looming election and what to do with a steel plant abandoned because of its age and profitability. The Brits looked at the bottom line and said, "Bye-bye, old chap." Smith looked at his election chances and made a fateful decision. The province of Nova Scotia would take over the steel mill and keep it running until the provincial government could find a buyer. Of course, they couldn't find a buyer and once the province had the mill it couldn't get rid of it.

Over the next several decades various governments tried different schemes to shore up Sydney Steel and stop the incredible money drain that ran into the millions and then billions. One executive after another was hired to modernize the old plant. Millions upon millions were spent. That executive would leave and another would arrive and a million more would go for other schemes. There was upgrading and downgrading, contraction and more contraction decade after decade, all accompanied with positive government press releases touting a new day for Sydney Steel and new markets that would soon be secured. Incredulous taxpayers looked on in disbelief.

Finally, over thirty years later, Premier John Hamm closed the plant, leaving behind billions of taxpayers' dollars and the biggest environmental quagmire in Canada, the Sydney Tar Ponds. More millions spent already on the tar ponds and many more millions to come.

With the wisdom of hindsight the adage was, "If they'd given every steelworker a million dollars and closed the plant in the

'60s, the taxpayers of Nova Scotia would have been better off and so would the steelworkers." Hindsight is wonderful, isn't it?

Crime

Halifax, of course, had crime in the '60s, just not the type you see today. We had no youth justice system and no roving gangs of juvenile delinquents cowardly swarming solitary victims. There was no such thing as a home invasion or taking guns to school, but there was theft and there was murder.

At CJ Radio we covered all aspects of murder: from the death of the victim to the arrest of the suspect, from the preliminary hearing to the actual trial. If there was a major murder trial underway, my work day was divided between an on-air shift and covering the trial. There were extensive preliminary hearings in those days, where the Crown presented its evidence to convince the court there was sufficient evidence to take the case forward to trial. Every piece of evidence to be presented at trial went through the preliminary hearing, including expert witnesses, every eyewitness, everybody who would be called to give testimony as well as all physical and circumstance evidence.

We covered the preliminary hearings and reported on them hourly by breathlessly running down the hall in the courthouse to the pay phone, giving a one-minute update on the events and testimony of the last hour. When the trial started, reporters knew the case, the evidence and the witnesses. Today the legal procedure is much more streamlined. Preliminary hearings have all but disappeared and so have reporters in private radio.

Pot, Weed, Marijuana

The big public inquiry of the era was the Le Dain Commission on the non-medical use of drugs. It was really about marijuana and what to do about its growing use in our society. According to some experts, pot smoking was sweeping the country. The Le Dain Commission took three long years, held hearings across Canada and produced a lengthy report that was described as thoughtful and thorough. The commission recommended cannabis be removed from the Narcotics Control Act and that provinces establish guidelines for possession and cultivation similar to those covering the use of alcohol.

Despite the money and time spent on the commission, its findings went up in smoke. The federal government ignored the recommendations, keeping marijuana illegal. In doing so, the government permitted the growth of large criminal empires that flourish to this day in Canada.

There isn't a person in Canada today who, if they so desire, can't acquire cannabis. It's even for sale on the Internet from several web sites that offer varying grades and varying prices. The Canadian marijuana crop is valued in the billions annually and taxpayers aren't getting a nickel from the profit. Instead, the money goes to biker gangs and other crime organizations. That profit has permitted them to become incredibly powerful. In some provinces marijuana is the most valuable cash crop. Besides, keeping marijuana illegal adds to its appeal, particularly among young people. If society wants to combat drugs it must make children knowledgeable about them, their impact, their effect, and what they do to the brain and the body. A knowledgeable nation is a forearmed nation. Education trumps legality every time.

Youth Justice

Those who complain about crime in Canada need only look at our recent past, from the lack of leadership in acting upon the best recommendations of the Le Dain Commission to the failure of our youth justice system. The handling of youth crime in Canada has been an unmitigated disaster. It is the puerile stepchild of the naive and ludicrous Young Offenders Act, leaving young people believing they are outside the law. Why wouldn't they feel they are immune from punishment? Instead of having the desired results against youth crime, it has had the opposite effect. It has fostered a growth, not a reduction, of young criminals, helped to enhance urban gangs and left youths with a hundred criminal offences on their record roaming the streets, feeling free to wreak havoc.

When home invasions came in vogue among criminals, Canadians were told there would be zero tolerance for this offence. As usual, that was all talk and nothing more.

I don't mean to suggest the answer to youth crime is necessarily more severe punishment or incarceration. What I do suggest is that intelligent discretion better serves society than a set of inflexible laws.

Sometimes, going back is actually striving ahead. I don't expect the social scientists or the dunderheads who designed the Young Offenders Act to agree, but I think we would be wise to scrap the entire youth justice apparatus. We appoint judges supposedly based on their intelligence and discretion. Let discretion prevail. The offender's age will always be a consideration in sentencing but how much of a consideration should be up to the judge, not be prescribed in legislation that restricts sentences and shields an offender's identity. Courts should be open and all offenders should be identified. The idea that not identifying a young offender will somehow help him or her out later in life is a pretty flimsy concept. It also negates the shame factor. Down through history, shame has always played a part in punishment. Destroying it hasn't helped either the young offender or society.

Mike Duffy

At CJCH Radio we not only covered crime, we covered everything. It was the last of the era when radio was king. We had a dozen people in our radio newsroom, on the air or on the beat or both. You'd find CJ reporters at Halifax City Council, Dartmouth City Council, Halifax County Council, at the legislature, committee meetings, major criminal trials and at news conferences. We did sports as well – minor baseball, hockey, college football and professional boxing. There was investigative reporting too. CJCH reporter Doug Harkness broke a major story on horrific conditions at the Cole Harbour Mental Hospital in Halifax County. That story garnered a national news award and public recognition.

I spent four years at CJ radio, starting on the night shift where I would deliver the news at five minutes to the hour and rush back to the newsroom to listen to CHNS, which was on the hour. If they had at story I missed at 8:00 I'd have it at 9:00 with voice clips from phone interviews. If I broke a story at 9:00 they'd have it at 10:00. We were young and very, very keen. I was promoted to the afternoon shift and later to mornings. I covered Dartmouth City Council and major murder trials and Halifax County Council.

The CHNS reporter who covered Halifax County Council was very good at his craft. There were many issues before county council and you had to figure out what was the most newsworthy while keenly listening to the discussions and writing your story for five to the hour. At the conclusion of the meetings I'd file my last report before driving back to the station. I'd have the opportunity to listen to my report at five to, and then switch to CHNS to hear my competitor. I was usually embarrassed by what I'd ignored and what the CHNS reporter had included. Of course, I didn't know at the time that I was competing against one of the best in the business. His name was Mike Duffy.

The Cast

After three years at CJ Radio, I was twenty-nine years old, news director and the voice of the morning news. "It's eight o'clock in the provincial capital; this is CJCH News, brought to you by Bob MacDonald Chevolet."

The newscast was chock full of local news with interview clips on crime, politics, traffic and an opinion piece with Edmund Morris. At 8:15 I'd be taping an interview for 8:30 and cutting tape for 8:55. I was engrossed in my profession, a radio man and loving it. It didn't seem possible that only a few short years ago I had been hanging lights and hitting Miss Ann on the head with a mike boom. It was the end of the golden era of radio. I've always been glad I was there to experience it. Radio news was king in those days but things were about to change forever.

Television Tricks

CHUM Toronto was getting ready to be a driving force in Maritime broadcasting. It had already purchased CJ Radio when I arrived there and a few years later bought CJCH television, as well as CKCW-TV in Moncton and CJCB Television in Sydney. The three stations would be turned into a mini network known as ATV. Other changes quickly followed, including the amalgamation of CJ radio and television news.

Television was becoming increasingly important as a news vehicle and had the potential to be vastly more profitable for the company. One of the first signs of the CJCH integration was the sudden transformation of a small radio announcer's booth into a tiny TV studio furnished with a table, telephone and a fixed camera. Sitting at the table in this booth you could look through two windows into the radio newsroom. The booth was to be used for a brief TV newscast in the mornings. My shift was the most compatible so I was given the job of reading this new TV mini newscast. I was back in television but this time with a shirt and tie, sitting under the lights instead of hanging them.

Even in the serious and competitive nature of the news business there were plenty of tricks played on the unsuspecting. On my second TV newscast I was the unsuspecting.

I considered the telephone on the desk of the newly fashioned TV studio to be merely a prop, until it started ringing while I was live on air. There was nothing in my background or training to cover such an eventuality. The ringing telephone was interrupting my broadcast and there was no video to hide behind. It was just me, the television camera and that damn phone. A thousand thoughts swept through my mind. It would look funny to take the receiver off the hook and leave it on the desk. What if it were a breaking story?

Beyond the camera I looked into the radio newsroom. Harris

Sullivan was holding a phone to his ear. Was he calling me? The phone rang again and again right in the middle of a story. I finally picked up the receiver and authoritatively said, "Hello."

"Bruce," – it was Harris's voice – "your fly is open."

I was speechless. The table I was sitting behind was high enough to expose my groin, something they never do to anchors today. A series of new concerns stampeded through my mind. Don't look down, I told myself. But, what if it were true? Harris sounded serious. What if I were unintentionally exposing myself to middle-aged housewives all over the Maritimes? What if PEI farmers, just in from the fields having a tea with the wife, were gaping at me? What if fishermen in Grand Manan, their boats snugly tied up at the wharf, were home watching television and killing themselves laughing? What if I was causing snickers in poolrooms and bemused comments in the nurses' residences or worse, snickers in the nurses' residences and bemused comments in poolrooms? Well, you know what I mean.

Don't look down, I silently screamed. Just continue reading.

But, but … do I want to be known as the guy who let it all hang out?

Don't look down. Just continue reading.

For God's sakes, man! You're on the air live. Get hold of yourself. No, don't. That's just a figure of speech.

If I am exposing myself, what would I do? Say excuse me, and pull up my fly? A zipper can be a dangerous instrument when handled hurriedly. Most men have had at least one painful experience with zippers and careless handling. Harris was a joker, a trickster. It wasn't true. Was it true?

There is something in the human psyche that ignores good advice even when you're giving it to yourself. I looked down. I was all right. I looked up, stared into the camera and since the story I was halfway through was totally lost, I said something like, "In other news today …"

Even though there were two walls and two soundproof windows between the booth and radio news, I could hear fits of hilarious laughter wafting through.

Because of the hijinks in radio, you learned never to leave your newscast unattended. In the announcer's booth where we read our casts, there was a slanted cork-topped table set at a steep angle to allow you to read without bending over, for better breathing and delivery. The cork prevented the papers from sliding. It was also readily acceptable to staples. Some joker would remove your top story and staple the rest of the newscast to the tabletop. You'd run back from the water fountain, jump into your chair as the news intro was playing, read your top story with bravado, move it from your stack of stories and see the rest of your cast stapled to the table. That trick was pulled on me my last day at CJ Radio. I remember trying to peel away little strips of paper between the staples to the next story. But in television, tricks were more costly to your career and reputation, since it was your face hanging out there.

Monkey Business

It's bad enough when your colleagues play tricks on you but when the animal kingdom gets involved it's just plain awful. This is another painful experience from my early days of the CJCH transition when I was not really "in" television but "on" television. I was picked to be one of the hosts of *ID*, the television supper show on CJCH. *ID* stood for In Depth. It was an hour-long interview show with several hosts including Bill Ozard, Harris Sullivan, Andrew Cochrane and myself. It was a great experience because you were dealing with a variety of subjects every night. It was all live, leaving open the possibility of many different experiences too. Jimmy Bell, who had more than one shot before arriving at the studio, fell asleep once during an interview. Another guest's chair – with him in it – fell on the riser. We had many interviews, many guests arriving and leaving the studio. Sometimes, with multiple hosts there were mix-ups. Bill Ozard, Harris Sullivan and I all had the embarrassing experience of sitting down with a guest and not even knowing his name, let alone why he was there.

Once, a travelling animal show came to town and I was assigned to interview the trainer. He brought a few of his animals along and we conducted the interview in the back parking lot, where we could roll the cameras to the end of the loading dock.

In the first minutes the interview was going well. The trainer was a gregarious guy and had no trouble talking. He had a rather large chimp with him and a rather aged lion and some other species from the wild kingdom. During the interview the chimpanzee took my hand and looked up at me endearingly.

"He likes you," said the trainer and I had to admit it was rather different doing an interview while holding hands with a chimpanzee. Then suddenly and totally unexpectedly, the chimp jumped right on my face, cradling my head with two very strong arms. The trainer tried to pry him off me but Mr. Chimpanzee wouldn't budge. Even though my face was completely covered by ape and my ears somewhat muffled by hairy arms, I could still hear the convulsive laughter of the cameramen. It took several seconds to extricate me from the chimp's embrace. By then the interview was in shambles, the cameramen couldn't control themselves and my face was burning and chafing from rough ape skin. The only good news was, we were out of time.

Suicide News Conference

There were plenty of unusual stories, such as the man who called the newsroom one night to tell us he was holding a news conference to announce his imminent death. He gave us an address in Mulgrave Park, just down the street from the station. When I arrived, other news cruisers were already parked outside. Sitting in the living room of his small apartment he calmly announced to the gathering media that he was going to commit suicide at 10 p.m.

When asked why, he responded simply by saying he didn't want to live anymore. Life, he said, held nothing for him and he was just tired of it all. He didn't say what you might expect him to say, that he was broke, jobless, had an incurable disease or his wife was leaving with the milkman. In fact, while he was holding his news conference with three or four microphones in his face, his wife was working away at the ironing board in the kitchen. She could hear every word but displayed no emotion. When asked about her husband's bizarre announcement, "It's up to him," she calmly said and refused further comment.

We reporters left perplexed and disturbed. The middle-aged man did not appear to be intoxicated and there was no odour of alcohol in the apartment. He would not disclose other details about his decision and I drove off wondering what to do with the story. Was it a story at all? If I ran it, would it force him to follow through on his decision? Before I got to the station, I had decided not to run the story. To my knowledge, no reporter ran the story and the man ultimately decided not to kill himself. Sometimes silence is golden.

Men in the Balloon

A great deal of money is spent annually in surveys and public relations research, trying to capture people's interest and imagination. Such market research is big business yet sometimes it happens naturally. Sometimes there is just a magic spark that lights fire to the public's imagination.

Very few events in the history of Halifax-Dartmouth captured the public's keen interest as did the story of two men who proposed to cross the Atlantic in a hot-air balloon. Mark Winters and Jerry Kostur came to town ready for the greatest adventure of their lives. They were preparing to attempt a transatlantic crossing. The chemistry of the time was just right for such a story of heroes and high adventure. Nova Scotia was ready to share vicariously in just such an exploit. With very little hype by the media, no initial publicity or advertising, there was immediate interest everywhere. People discussed the possibility of success in taverns and coffee shops, at lunch counters and over backyard fences. Was it a hair-brained scheme? Could a world record be set? Could these brazen young men be the first to cross the Atlantic in a balloon?

In the hot summer of 1968, both Halifax radio stations jumped into the growing interest and tried to corner the market on the event. CHNS ran a contest to name the balloon – eventually it was called the Maple Leaf. At CJ Radio we did interviews with the balloonists, ran stories day and night, sought public reaction and discussed their chances of making it all the way to England or Ireland or wherever they might land. CJCH offered its large television studio as a facility for the balloonists to attach a protective Mylar cover over their balloon. The silver cover would help to keep the heat inside and make the balloon less susceptible to atmospheric conditions. To attach the overlay, they used an adhesive similar to rubber cement. The pungent fumes were so strong most of us were light-headed. So we damaged our brains. This was high adventure.

The launch was set for the second week in August. Thousands turned out to witness the historic event. Roads leading to the launch site at Cow Bay were backed up as far as the eye could see; extra police tried to deal with the volume of traffic. Entire families arrived with picnic lunches and blankets and Grandmother. All other events in metropolitan Halifax-Dartmouth were forgotten. There wasn't another story anywhere. It was the balloon, the balloonists, the launch, the adventure, the excitement. The rest of the world simply disappeared.

We put a lot of effort into our coverage. We would report the launch from land, sea and air. My assignment was to follow the balloon in a twin-engine Apache aircraft from the launch site out over the Atlantic, giving minute by minute updates on its progress.

Inflating the balloon took a long time. As we flew over the site high above the crowd, the balloon slowly transformed from a lumpy silver heap scattered haphazardly on the ground to a great silver dome rising skyward. Thousands cheered as the balloon finally became erect, ready to challenge the heavens and set a new world record.

The balloonists climbed into the gondola, waved to the cheering throng. Then there was the dramatic moment of liftoff. The silver ball, finally free and unfettered, suspended unmoving at first, then slowly rose up and over the water. Away it soared from the cheering crowd. People waved handkerchiefs, fathers held their children up in the air so they could witness humanity's latest attempt to challenge the Atlantic.

The two pilots, cameraman Wayne Clark and I trailed the balloon for many miles high above billowy clouds and gliding seabirds. I filed reports until the red glow of dusk told us it was time to turn back. I did my last report describing the image of the silver ball drifting away into the Atlantic haze. It was a beautiful sight, I told my listeners. One you don't forget.

We celebrated our great coverage. The management was happy and we knew we'd done a good job. However, the celebration and the night were short. I was roused from my bed by an urgent phone call at three in the morning. The balloon had ditched in the ocean. The balloonists had been picked up by a fishing boat. We had already hired another boat and I was to intercept the balloonists in the ocean for interviews before they reached land. We caught up to them miles off the coast, where I boarded the fishing boat and conducted my first interview for the national news. I got plenty of tape and film and got their story firsthand while every detail of the experience was fresh in their minds. Upon coming into Halifax, who did I see standing on the dock looking rather dishevelled? Mike Duffy. In some small way it made up for being beaten at county council.

Stuffing Ballot Boxes for Angus L.

We were good at digging up news. We were muckrakers too, not a newsroom that existed on press releases and fluffy interviews. For young keeners it was disheartening to finally come up against another company of people who were neither as driven nor as idealistic as we were.

That revelation came in the 1970 Nova Scotia election campaign. Vote buying was a common practice in Nova Scotia. It was one of those things no one really talked about and the passive newspapers usually turned a blind eye. At CJ we deliberately set out to throw a spotlight into this dark corner of Nova Scotia. Reporter Steve Kimber enlisted a man who would act as our agent in the field. We actually got him on tape accepting a bribe for his vote from a Liberal Party worker.

A good story, but one that could have dire consequences for the company if we weren't absolutely correct in every aspect of our revelation. It was the type of story you needed to run past the company lawyers. Our lawyer was prominent Halifax Liberal John McInnis. He was also a shareholder in CJCH and sat on the board of directors. McInnis not only wouldn't let us run the story but heartily criticized the very idea of turning the spotlight on something as common and practical as vote buying. When we pleaded our case on the dishonesty and impropriety of the situation, he snapped, "So what? I stuffed ballot boxes for Angus L."

I believe he did. I also thought he was a dinosaur, failing to see the enlightenment of our modern world.

We had spent time and effort on the vote buying story and we were bucked by the company, who argued that dishonesty was fine. We argued corruption in Nova Scotia was seldom brought to light and we could break the silence and bring Nova Scotia politics up to a higher standard. We had evidence on tape of a party official (I believe it was a Liberal) offering the bribe but the Tories did the same thing. It was the political culture and we were dejected that nothing would come of all our efforts. The status quo prevailed and as usual the Establishment ruled. We could break all the stories we wanted until we got too close to somebody's self-interest. When that happened, investigative reporters could go to hell. The situation left me with the first taste of resentment for my industry. It was the beginning of my mistrust of officialdom and the high rollers, institutions and agencies that control our lives.

Personal events were weighing on me as well. My marriage had disintegrated with alarming rapidity. I was left emotionally wretched. In addition, the sands of my employment were shifting under my feet. We had a major shuffle at the station. The integration of radio news into the television operation was complete by 1971. Bill Ozard had moved from radio manager to news director of the combined radio-TV operation and I was given a split shift, reading the 6:00 p.m. news on television while still doing early mornings on radio. I was working from six in the morning until seven at night. Such hours are probably illegal under today's labour laws and if they're not, they should be. After four years of great energy and enthusiasm, I was making mistakes, missing stories. I had lost my edge. I knew it was time to move on. Two of the CJ staff, Thompson MacDonald and Barry Horne, had already left for Calgary. In the spring of 1972 I followed them into the golden west.

6

Calgary, 1972

CFCN Radio

CFCN Radio and Television sits on a hill overlooking the city of Calgary. The first time I walked into the newsroom it was a Saturday afternoon. I had arrived the night before and a phone call directed me to the West Gate tavern on the Bow Trail. The news staff was having a bash for departing news director Ian Parker, who was moving to Toronto. It was hardly what you would call an intimate setting. The West Gate was bigger than any drinking establishment in the Maritimes, holding hundreds of boisterous patrons. One of Parker's last official acts was hiring me, for which I was eternally grateful. Over a cold beer we arranged to meet the next day when I would be given a tour of the station and sign my employment papers.

The newsroom was empty that Saturday afternoon. The rows of empty desks gave the place a rather desolate look. One man was standing at the far end of the room with his back to me. His suit coat was open and his hands were on his hips. He was peering through the glass into the television studio as if he was waiting for someone. As I approached he turned and gave me a broad smile. "Hi," he said, "I'm Peter Lougheed."

Aside from the news staff, the first person I met in Alberta was the premier, there to tape an interview. In the following months I would see him on the campaign trail, not walking but running from house to house. I've covered many political campaigns, federal, provincial and municipal, and I've watched many a candidate go door to door. Peter Lougheed was the only one who ran, a political marathoner making every second count.

A few months after our meeting, I was picked to co-anchor the Alberta election on CFCN Radio. I got the job, I guess, because most of my colleagues were tied up with television. Once the polls closed, the results started coming in fast and furious. The Lougheed Tories built up such a commanding lead my co-anchor and I began predicting Tory victories in one seat after another. Provincial election coverage usually takes two to three hours. Sometimes they're cliff-hangers, going down to the last seat where the results are very close and you're on the air till midnight. Not that night in Calgary. An hour after the polls closed our broadcast was over. The Progressive Conservatives under Peter Lougheed had swept every seat in the province. I never witnessed anything like it again.

A Western Awakening

Calgary is a city populated by people from other places. The daily life of the town is carried out by people from Moose Jaw or Winnipeg, Toronto or the interior of British Columbia. To an easterner unaccustomed to western culture, the most jarring aspect of western Canadian cities was the total disregard for Aboriginal people of the prairies.

On my first official work day, photographer Jack Kalafa gave me a tour of the downtown area so I could familiarize myself with my new surroundings. We drove past city hall and my eyes opened wide. Half a dozen bodies were sprawled on the lawn, resembling the grim battlefield scenes of lifeless warriors cut down in the heat of combat with arms and legs splayed. Some were on their backs while others lay face down on the grass. They were sprawled haphazardly on the walkway up to the front door of Calgary City Hall – an incongruous scene in the setting of a modern city.

"Who are those people?" I asked.

"Indians," was Jack's reply, said without hostility, embarrassment or resignation.

"They're drunk," he added.

Men in business suits walked by without noticing. So did woman and cowboys. They all passed and never cast a sideways glance at the bodies on the grass. Intoxicated Aboriginals were simply part of the urban landscape. They were an invisible people and the popular mentality was that if they drifted into town from their reservation, well, what can we do? When the Olympics came to Calgary, the city sanitized itself and all the undesirables were swept up and hidden so visitors couldn't see the sordid side of city life.

I wasn't in Calgary for the Olympics. The lifeless bodies weren't either.

Ralph Kline

As a general reporter for both radio and television and with no specific beat, I covered anything and everything from South Dakota to the Rockies. CFCN news had a large staff, with reporters competing to get their stories on the air. You were required to dig up your story ideas for the morning assignment meeting where the day's work was doled out. If your ideas weren't accepted or, as more often happened, another reporter had the same idea and got to the bosses first, you might be left without an assignment. If that was the case you were discouraged from hanging around the newsroom. No news director wants the general manager dropping in to observe idle hands sitting around the shop slurping coffee.

The mantra went like this: "If you don't have an assignment, go out and find one. Dig around and come up with something good enough to get on the six o'clock news. You're a reporter, aren't you? Hit the streets and come back when you have something. But stay in touch in case we need you."

On days without an assignment I would wander downtown to our city hall bureau where things were very relaxed. Our city hall reporter was an affable guy. Because he had the city hall beat he didn't have to attend assignment meetings or come up with a story idea or two every day. He would simply phone in what was happening at city hall, the important meetings scheduled and what he was most likely going to be filing for 6 p.m. He was the only reporter to have his own little sanctum – an escape from the bedlam of the newsroom. His name was Ralph Kline.

Ralph and I became good friends and broke a lot of bread together, hitting the high points in the city and a few of the rather low spots too. Ralph was a Calgary kid. I was always amazed how many people he knew. Walking in downtown Calgary with Ralph Kline was an experience even before he entered politics. He was already the statesman of the streets. I wasn't surprised when he was victorious in his bid for mayor of Calgary. Nor was it startling news that he won handily, even though his campaign budget was puny compared to his opponent's.

The Oil Patch

Despite cattle pens and a robust agricultural sector just outside its boundaries, Calgary was then, as it is now, very much an oil town. Oil flowed through the veins of the city's business life. The law firms and accounting firms and the firms involved in distribution, exploration, technical mapping and supply were all involved in the oil patch. There were oil men on city council. Oil men were the movers and shakers who hung out with other oil men. Their main hangout was Calgary's Petroleum Club. As a reporter, I quickly learned that more than a few members took extremely long lunches. Maybe they were conducting business or maybe they were getting sloshed (probably both), but if you had an interview with someone from the oil patch you better get it before lunch. Don't get me wrong, there were some hard-working people in the oil business, but you felt some people on the periphery of the industry were more players than workers.

Military Stories

There were plenty of military stories in Alberta too and there is hardly a square mile of the province I didn't cover that year. I always seemed to be going somewhere, from Cold Lake to the United States border. Extensive training was carried out at Suffield near North Dakota, where British and other Commonwealth troops came to polish their battle skills in the wide-open terrain. These exercises often prompted noisy protests from people who thought the world already had enough of war. I was sent to Suffield to cover the military exercises sometimes and at other times to cover protests and peace rallies.

At the other end of the province, at the Cold Lake air base, it was all about flying. Along with photographer Morris Cruise, I was assigned to do a story on the risky business of aerial refuelling. The military was teaching its pilots to fill their fuel tanks in midair to save time during long-distance surveillance when fuel, airfields and bases might not be available. The CF5 had extremely short legs, which was one of the reasons it wasn't the fighter jet the military wanted. But since politics plays the big hand in military procurement, it's the one they got.

Aerial refuelling gave the CF5 the ability to cover more territory without landing but the downside is the danger. It's a tricky business and thrilling to observe up close, as pilots maneuver these small fighter jets under the wings of the large 707 tanker aircraft. It's like sex in the air – the pilot has to negotiate his fuel valve into the opening of the 707's tank while both aircraft are travelling at six hundred miles an hour. It takes skill and hours of practice. I sat fascinated, watching the procedure as the fighter jet maneuvered into position under the bigger plane's wing. One slip could cause a major disaster. Often, pilots missed at first and moved away to come back for another try. Filming this ritualistic mating dance in the sky, cameraman Cruise strapped into his seat in the jet was the victim of a G-force severe enough to drive the eye piece into his eye. That wasn't as bad as vomiting into his oxygen mask. I have a lot of appreciation for the people who take pictures.

Alone on the Night Shift

From a journalism perspective, my most noteworthy contribution to Calgary was a series of stories we did on the death of a teenager. The boy was murdered while working the night shift in a small convenience store. I certainly wasn't the only reporter working on the story, but I contributed a lot of the work. Our reports drew attention to the vulnerability of such employees and contributed to a change in Alberta legislation, requiring two clerks per shift at nights. Other provinces would have been wise to do the same. That boy died but our stories may have saved a number of other lives.

The Talk Show

One of my best experiences at CFCN was hosting the radio talk show for several weeks. The show had a good following. Its long-time host requested a leave of absence to look after his ailing wife. I was surprised when the management asked me to fill in during his absence. They didn't have to ask me twice. Because I had always read the news over the years on the Halifax talk show at CJCH radio – Halifax hosts included Bill Ozard, John Gilbert, Eileen Stubbs, Frank Fillmore, Ron Pumphreys, Pat Blanford, Marvin Burke and more – I never had the opportunity to actually do the "talk." However, I'd seen enough hosts up close to know what made a good one and how to avoid being mediocre.

As I expected, it was a thoroughly enjoyable experience. I loved setting up the subject in the opening minutes each day, pulling out snippets of ideas from the morning headlines and seeing what grabbed the listeners' interest, then building the show around that topic. I had an assistant to contact news-makers or authorities on any subject. That added an air of authenticity but I used them sparingly. This was a people's program and there was never a dull day. If nothing grabbed the listening audience all I had to do was say the magic word and the bank of phone lines lit up like a Christmas tree. The magic word in western Canada in 1972 was, of course, "Trudeau."

Pierre Trudeau

Today Pierre Trudeau is a Canadian hero well on his way to being indelibly stamped as a revered icon of the country. In the early '70s, particularly, but not exclusively, in western Canada he was the national nemesis, a lefty Liberal with a flower in his lapel. He wore sandals and open-necked shirts. Even worse, he was promoting the French language. He was recruited into federal politics by Lester Pearson as one of the so-called three wise men. The other alleged wise guys were Marc LaLonde and Gerard Pelletier.

As justice minister in the Pearson government Trudeau spearheaded the drive to overhaul the criminal code. He was famous for his oft-quoted quip, "The government has no place in the bedrooms of the nation."

When he campaigned for the Liberal leadership he had the aura of a rock star. There was a blaze of public adoration seldom seen before. Huge crowds showed up at airports when he arrived. Men applauded, women wildly cheered or wept. They called him handsome or cute and they said he had charisma. He was a bachelor and rich and on and on and ...

Trudeau was a star, all right, a political novelty like no other. Still, in politics you have critics. Those who disliked him for his style called him haughty and arrogant.

As many have learned when reaching power, politics can be a bitter pill. The longer Trudeau was in power the more his philosophy was in contradiction to his policies. He believed in civil liberties but implemented the War Measures Act in October 1970, turning the country into a police state. People were roused from their beds by police in the middle of the night and whisked away to jail in acts reminiscent of Nazi Germany.

When his popularity plummeted as it was bound to do, the pendulum of public opinion swung hard the other way and Pierre Trudeau was berated and hated. He flip-flopped on economic policy too, at first permitting a growth in government and spending, then cutting jobs and slashing services to keep that spending under control.

In the end, Pierre Trudeau was a politician as fickle to the times he lived in as anyone else. Some of the criticism concerning him was justified and some was just petty. He did more than any leader to promote the French language and bring Quebec into the mainstream of Canadian life. He also repatriated our constitution, making us a country in our own right.

What other Canadian prime minister ever caused such a furor over his style? There were articles in newspapers on Trudeau's attire. The only time Joe Clark's clothing hit the news was when it was tucked away in his luggage, lost on an overseas flight. Bob Stanfield attained attire befuddlement when he tucked his pants into cowboy boots and lost support in the west. Mackenzie King may have seen images in his shaving mug and occasionally taken direction on policy from his dead mother, but like most prime ministers he dressed in drab respectability. Can you picture Stephen Harper in an ascot and sandals?

Trudeau was different and now that he's gone, so is the animosity towards him. There is nothing like death to vanquish loathing.

The Happy Hooker

Calgary also gave me my first major insight into how far afield the media could stray by turning an unimportant event into headline news.

When Xaviera Hollander, the Happy Hooker, came to town to promote her book by the same name, the collective media of Calgary tittered in giddy anticipation that turned into a frenzy of coverage. Every radio and television station interviewed her. The red carpet, if not literally, then figuratively, was rolled out as if she were the Queen. CFCN went out of its way to accommodate her, cancelling other studio events to conduct a special interview with Xaviera, so copywriters and studios crews eagerly awaited her arrival. No other author in the world would have been accorded such special treatment. The entire city media had turned into a tabloid.

I read a quotation by Nancy J. Woodhull from The Freedom Forum recently that said, "Attack journalism and tabloid journalism have their place. They get things out in the open. Once they are out in the open, the media have a responsibility to try and give the story perspective that has real meaning."

In Calgary there was plenty of euphoria but very little perspective. I didn't go into the studio with the rest of the staff to watch her being interviewed. Maybe I was just being a prig, too strongly attached to my Protestant roots. I thought the entire hoopla a farce. It was also a lie. I'd spent enough time on the streets to see that very few hookers were actually happy. How could you be happy in a life of violence, pimps, drugs and disease? What was really going on was media manipulation on a large scale. And the media, acting as if it had just discovered sex, not only loved the manipulation, it wanted more.

Later in my life when I was teaching media courses, I would use The Happy Hooker story as an example of how the media can get caught up in the excitement it had helped create. How one station feeds off another, hyping the pitch higher and higher until ultimately the unimportant becomes a major event. In 1931, Mary Day Winn wrote, "The collective intelligence of any group of people who are thinking as a herd rather than individually is no higher than the intelligence of the stupidest members."

Amen.

The Late Offer

I only spent a year in Calgary but what a remarkable year it was. In twelve short months I had a wide array of experiences and adventures. If CFCN had offered me the radio talk show I would have stayed in Calgary. I liked the city and I liked the news staff. They were full of life and fun. The station was owned by Maclean

Hunter, good people to work for and my job was extremely varied and interesting. But in 1973 I received an offer I couldn't refuse.

It was an opportunity to become a television news supervisor, the chance not only to run my own television newsroom but also the chance to participate in transforming an antiquated television operation into a modern news enterprise. The challenge was irresistible.

As I was settling into a new life in Winnipeg, CFCN called and offered me the permanent position of host of the Calgary talk show. I had made a commitment to a new employer and I had to turn down a job I really wanted. That's how life works out sometimes.

7

Winnipeg, 1973

CKY

Winnipeg is the most underrated city in Canada. Although its winters are perishingly cold, the weather the rest of the year beats that of most places. It's also as different from Calgary as day is from night. In the early '70s, Calgary was an oil town trying to cling to its disappearing cowtown roots. It was too new for much history and too rural for much culture. As western cities go, Winnipeg is old, cultured and extremely multinational in its population. Nobody wears cowboy hats in Winnipeg and instead of a stampede as their annual event, they have a multicultural festival. Winnipeg is the west but it looks and sounds like the east.

As with most western cities, Winnipeg was established at the confluence of two rivers. The Red and Assiniboine played an important role in the fur trade; what followed was Fort Gary, Rupertsland, Louis Riel, grain and trains. Winnipeg had time to refine itself with large ethnic communities that are more diverse than the newer oil and cowboy culture of Calgary.

CKY Radio and Television were located in Polo Park near the Winnipeg Arena and football stadium. The newsroom was in a windowless basement and the major newscast was still using black and white film. The station was owned by Moffat Communications. Well-known Alberta newsman Dale O'Hara had done a good job for the company's radio station in Calgary and been hired to take over the Winnipeg radio and television newsrooms. His background was all radio and he gave me the task of transforming the television operation into a more competitive news-gathering operation. CKY's major television newscast at six was getting killed in the ratings. It lacked resources and manpower. The rich and powerful CBC Winnipeg, which had been the news leader since the advent of television, had a virtual death grip on the ratings.

My first task was to study the market and find the best way to improve and update the newsroom, both in our news-gathering ability and the "look" of the on-air program. After all, television news is a blend of show business and journalism. Unfortunately, you can't ignore one aspect without consequences to the other. If you ignore the journalism your program is void of substance, an empty vessel. If you ignore the show business side, which is really the television aspect, your program looks visually uninteresting. Getting the right blend is the challenge and the dilemma for all news directors. That's television.

Some of the conclusions in those early days were easy. We needed more people, an expanded coverage and total colour. Our first major purchases were a Jamieson coloured film processor from Texas and new film cameras. O'Hara and I went on recruiting trips to Saskatchewan, looking at local talent we could bring to CKY.

More than anything during my first weeks in Winnipeg, I was surprised at how hostile the newspapers were to television in general and to CKY in particular. There seemed to be an ongoing grudge toward the television station or its owners, the Moffat family. That hostility intensified when we made some major changes to our on-air staff.

One of those changes concerned long-time sportscaster Cactus Jack Wells. He was a character whose reputation was far mightier than his ratings. In 1973 there wasn't a great deal of effort going into Cactus Jack's work. I don't blame him for this. After all, how many years can one repeat the same performance without the image beginning to tarnish? On-air people are like politicians: they don't know when to step off the stage. Dale O'Hara, radio news supervisor Wayne Bill and I spent considerable time discussing the situation. Cactus Jack was an institution in Winnipeg. More famous than his broadcasts was the fact he got in a fistfight with the coach of the Winnipeg Blue Bombers after a Grey Cup game. That dust-up received wide press coverage. The altercation was very public, embellishing Cactus Jack's reputation, if not his ratings. The newspapers did what we expected when we fired Cactus Jack. They wrote a number of snide comments at our efforts to improve the on-air product.

Bill Cosby

So that's how it was in 1973. We were far behind in the television ratings, cursed in the newspapers and ignored by most of the public. Frankly, we needed to get people's attention and the best way to get more people to watch your television station was to put more people on the air. We started a series of ads where we took our cameras on the streets and asked people if they had noticed a difference in CKY news. Some of the answers were positive and some were negative. The negative responses were more priceless than the positive ones. Many were humorous and they had definite promotional value. The promos developed into a regular series where we took our cameras on the streets for opinion and reactions to various news stories. The practice is common today but was seldom done in the early '70s and it encouraged people to pay attention.

Bill Cosby helped out too. The popular comedian was doing a show in Winnipeg and we asked him to do a spontaneous news promo for us. Cosby smiled, rolled up a newspaper, looked at the camera and said with that wonderful, mischievous expression of his, "Every time I'm in Winnipeg I smoke CKY News." It didn't make any sense and that was part of its allure, and it was Bill Cosby saying CKY News. We were getting talked about.

Our next job was to earn their respect by doing some good, hard-nosed journalism.

The Slum Lords

The story that helped us do that fell into our lap while we were covering a family literally kicked into the street. The house they were being evicted from was substandard in the extreme, from the walls to the floors to the plumbing. In fact, it wasn't fit for human habitation.

I instructed my reporter to find out who owned the dilapidated property. It turned out to be a wealthy businessman living in one of the city's exclusive neighbourhoods. I sent a reporter to get an interview but no one would answer the door. We had shots of the reporter standing on the doorstep of this white mansion and knocking, to no avail. We used that film on the news that night as well as the film of the slum house.

Then it hit me. Winnipeg had many slum houses with people living in awful conditions. Let's take the worst houses in Winnipeg, put them on the air and show the houses of the people responsible for them. We were exposing the slumlords of the city: lawyers, business executives, the people with power and clout.

By that time I had begun nightly news commentaries, what you might call another barb in the underbelly of the Establishment, particularly the slumlords hiding behind a cloak of respectability. The worst types were those who preyed on the elderly. Six old men were discovered living in incredible filth in a house worse than a hovel.

Commentary: April 1974

With all the provincial agencies, volunteer groups, church people, service clubs and all other goodwill gathering throughout the city of Winnipeg, how could these six men find themselves in such a state of affairs in 1974? But there they were, living amongst the vermin, filth and urine that characterized their former residence on Talbot Avenue.

And what about the landlord? Will he go scot-free? Where were the health inspectors? Someone somewhere should be answerable.

The problem in this case is not unique. There are other homes in Winnipeg, just as filthy, where greedy landlords are willing to take pension money from elderly people and let them live in dirt and grime. It seems the time is long overdue for a new type of agency to deal strictly with slum landlords, and don't tell me we're dealing with them now because we're not. Just take a look at the men who lived on Talbot Avenue.

* * *

To say the shit hit the fan was an understatement, but Moffat Communications stood its ground and backed us up. The story set the tone for CKY News. We might use silly promos but we were a no-nonsense newsroom ready to take on the city's elite.

City Hall

Winnipeg was a city full of political intrigue. There was a large city council that was fractious in the extreme. Unlike most municipal governments, party politics at Winnipeg City Hall was very much out in the open. A large and boisterous group of city councillors had their own party – the Independent Citizens Election Committee, known as the ICEC. It was born out of discontent with the working of municipal government and the status quo. City council meetings were vocal, verbal, loud and argumentative. It was at such a meeting that councillor Slaw Rebchuck voiced his now famous remark that lives in the annals of Canadiana: "A verbal agreement isn't worth the paper it's written on."

There was always news coming from city hall, always stories and controversies. The long-time mayor was Steve Juba. I remember he once came into the station for an interview. We were leaning against the editing table watching the Watergate hearings.

"You know," he said to me, "there's a lot of dishonesty down there and the same thing could be going on here."

This was a strange thing to say to a news director when his city was embroiled in one controversy after another. Was it, I wondered, a subtle signal to keep digging and dig even deeper? I don't know what Winnipeg city council meetings are like today but in those days they were the best show in town, with some of the best performers too.

Bus Stop Buddy

Winnipeg was a union town. At one time it was in the grip of a city-wide transit strike. Reporter Marshall Armstrong came up with the idea of helping people get around the inconvenience, with our help. We launched a program called Bus Stop Buddies. People filled out a short application and we confirmed their identity then gave them a large card with Bus Stop Buddy on it. People with cars put the card on their dashboards and people without wheels stood in bus stops and held out the cards so they could be picked up. With no transit buses on the roads, traffic moved around the city much faster than usual and everybody appreciated our efforts, except, of course, the striking bus drivers who called us anti-union – among other unmentionable names.

I was enjoying myself in Winnipeg. I moved my wife and daughter into a small house in the River Heights section of the city. It was a great neighbourhood with tree-lined streets near parks and playgrounds. My daughter Leslie was already old enough for school, which was nearby. Next door were Rita and Gord McGregor. They were great neighbours and the long summer evenings were filled with barbeques and socializing. Winnipeg had theatre and art, but what really made the city was the diversity of its ethnic communities and how well they got along. Folklarama was the annual festival that celebrated the city's various cultures. You could buy a passport, get on a bus and ride from pavilion to pavilion tasting the food and drink of the different countries Winnipeg neighbourhoods represented. It was great fun and something to look forward to each year. The people of Winnipeg were genuine, hard-working and as polite as people anywhere. Here's an example of what I mean.

Commentary, December 1973: Politeness Capital of Canada

Last night while driving home from work, something rather unusual happened, which just revealed some pretty good insight into the people of Winnipeg. I was in a line of traffic waiting for the light to change to flashing green so I could make a turn. The light changed but the first car in line, apparently from out of the city, didn't turn. I guess the driver was waiting for a green arrow. Then the lights changed again and the line of traffic grew longer as we waited through another red light. Again the light turned green, meaning those of us in the turning lane could go, but again the first car in the line waited. This happened through three lights, yet never a car horn sounded. Finally, the driver directly behind the slowpoke got out of his vehicle and informed the motorist when he should turn.

I couldn't help wondering what would have happened if this were Montreal or Toronto or any other large city. It has struck me from time to time that people in Winnipeg can keep their cool and have more manners in public than any group I've ever seen. And it might not be a bad idea as we go into official centennial celebrations to promote Winnipeg as the politeness capital of Canada. In these days of big city hustle and bustle, it is indeed a rare distinction.

* * *

In the intervening years, politeness and civility have waned. As we are dished up daily doses of culture from south of the border, we slowly become more Americanized in our attitudes and, unfortunately, in our aggression. My hope is Winnipeg hasn't lost its distinctiveness or its manners.

Crime

Like all urban areas, Winnipeg had its dark side, its underbelly of drugs and crime. There was poverty, suicide, political cronies and crooked deals. A monster called the Balaclava Rapist terrified people in my neighbourhood by hiding in their garages, waiting for a woman to drive in alone. He committed a number of sexual assaults before he was apprehended.

One particularly heinous crime stands out in my memory of those Winnipeg years. A young woman was forced to walk along a road on a winter night after her car broke down. She was picked up by a stranger, who drove her to a deserted spot outside of the city, where he raped her and then almost beat her to death. She was repeatedly stabbed in the face with a wooden stake. He left her unconscious in the snow, fully expecting her to die. But the will to live is extremely strong. The victim, bleeding badly and barely alive, crawled through snowy brush. The night was freezing as only Winnipeg nights can be. Blood was pouring from her face and she would have died had it not been for a dog. The dog, let out for an evening pee, heard her crawling through the bush. The dog started barking and the farmer located her.

Because the crime occurred outside the city limits, it was the RCMP's jurisdiction and I got to know two young Mounties working on the case. They followed a lot of dead-end leads. The woman was terribly traumatized and couldn't identify much about the man or his car except she thought she remembered seeing the word Datsun on his dash.

"Every time we get discouraged," one of the Mounties told me, "we go back to her hospital room and just look at her. That one look fires us up again."

The man was finally captured. As a child, he had apparently been badly beaten by his father, so because of what his lawyer called "the unusual circumstances of his life," he was sentenced to less than ten years in penitentiary.

After a very long period of convalescence, the woman recovered but the physical scars and the trauma of that night will remain with her always.

The early '70s were a tumultuous time for the RCMP. The Mounties were involved in a number of scandals that received national attention, including opening people's mail and even burning a barn in Quebec. Their internal procedures and organizations were far out of date. I was hammering the Mounties pretty hard in some of my television commentaries, never believing that thirty years later they'd still be in a state of disarray and eventually appoint their first civilian commissioner.

Commentary, May 1974: Time for a Change in the RCMP

The number of Mounties who turned up for union discussions probably raised a few eyebrows in the commissioner's office. While techniques in criminology have taken giant strides in the past couple of decades, rules and regulations for the RCMP are a century behind. Imagine having to wear spurs while doing highway patrol! You can dig them into your seat all you want but the car won't go any faster.

What about violations of civil rights, the grievance procedure and disciplinary action? Even military tribunals allowed those charged to have legal counsel. Also, Mounties can only appeal to the same group that meted out disciplinary action in the first place. Hardly fair. Hardly just.

With these last-century regulations, it's small wonder there's friction in the ranks of the RCMP. Someone should tell the commissioner's office this is 1974 and our legal system is based on fair hearings and the right to counsel. If it's good enough for the rest of us, it's good enough for the RCMP.

* * *

The public didn't react favourably to such commentaries. People didn't like to hear negative comments about their national police force. It was one image of Canada they wanted to remain untarnished, as pristine as the brass buttons on the red coats during the Musical Ride. However, members of the force wanted to hear more of my commentaries. When I moved on to other subjects for a few nights, the two young constables working on the rape case came into my office, inquiring why I wasn't talking about the force anymore. They wanted to keep the heat on the brass in order to bring about badly needed changes.

You would think the force would have changed by then but they unfortunately didn't. To make matters worse, in 1995 Disney

Corporation purchased the right to market toys and other products incorporating the image of the Canadian red-coated Mountie. After a long history of difficulty in regulating its own image, the RCMP decided to sell its symbolic identification to a world leader in profit-based management. Make a ceramic red-coated Mountie and expect a letter from Mickey Mouse! That contract ran out in 2000.

Dirty Movies

We received reports that a movie house on Portage Avenue was showing adult films that people said were really pornographic. We thought it might be interesting to set up a camera on the sidewalk outside the theatre and interview patrons who had just seen the movie. It was one of the funniest moments I've ever seen on television.

What we found leaving the theatre from an afternoon matinee, almost exclusively, was a group of very old men. They were neither timid talking about nor ashamed to be seen leaving a girlie film. In fact, they were willing to speak freely. They resembled a collection of comedians such as George Burns doing his best stand-up routine.

It's been many years since that day and I can't be specific about their exact comments. But one old guy, with a face that looked as if it had lived three lives, was asked if he thought the movie was pornographic. In the throaty croak of an octogenarian he answered, "I don't know, but I'd like to have that girl for two or three hours."

Digging Up Bones

CKY covered much of Manitoba with transmitters reaching far into the northern part of the province. I hired reporter Jim Burke to specialize in stories about the north, where thousands of Canada's original people lived. These native people made up a significant percentage of the population but were mostly invisible to the media. Jim knew the north and made several trips to the far-flung corners of the province.

His most horrendous discovery was of a work crew digging through an old Native cemetery, strewing bones and pieces of coffins on the ground and leaving the human remains uncovered. It was such a startling lack of respect that we made a big deal out of it. Even though we had pictures to prove our story, Winnipeg newspapers as usual paid little attention to the discovery, filling their pages with lesser fare.

Nightly Commentaries

I tried to cover every situation in my commentaries – not just the awful truth but the weird and funny too. If you just have an angry rant every night, people will soon get sick of listening to you. You need balanced material, reasoned thought and a degree of entertainment. A good commentator has to do more than criticize. The most positive aspect of commentaries is to suggest solutions to social problems and public policy. If you're lucky and good at what you do, most of the suggested solutions come from the viewing public. I've learned long ago that by and large, people have more common sense than politicians. Those in elected office have to see things through the haze of party politics, always with an eye to getting re-elected.

Some of the Winnipeg stories were simply bizarre. Such was the story of the motorist who had a car accident in the town of Steinbach. A man wanted to report his accident, but for love nor money, he couldn't find a policeman.

Commentary: Policemen's Holiday

Maybe the people of Steinbach know what to do when the side of their car gets creamed by a motorist who didn't stop, but a Winnipeg man was visiting that town last night and his first thought was to find a policeman. Sounds easy, but in Steinbach it is difficult. He went to the police station. Nobody there. He went to a telephone booth and tried phoning the police. There was a recorded reply telling him to phone back in the morning. He went to the RCMP detachment. There were three cruisers in the parking lot but nobody answered the doorbell. He gave up, returned to Winnipeg and this morning, shortly after eight o'clock, he phoned the town police. He was informed the police weren't in and told to leave a message because they do check in periodically.

Police finally got his message some eight and a half hours after he discovered his damaged car. There are five members on the Steinbach police force, plus the RCMP detachment. My question is, what happens in Steinbach if there's an emergency? I think that's the question the people of Steinbach should be asking as well.

* * *

Needless to say, I was not always popular with the police or officialdom generally. My boss at CKY was Jim Purves, the station's general manager and one of the two best bosses I've ever had. He believed in news and defended me even though I stretched his patience at times. But there was one story where even he couldn't help me. That was when CKY found itself in the news in a rather negative way.

It had to do with a scandal and a travel agency, which just so happened to be at least partly owned by Moffat, the station owner. Of course, we covered the story, digging harder than ever to show we didn't hold back, even in our own corporate family. The company lawyer and I had been at loggerheads as the company was already taking lots of flak over our news operation. While I was out of town, Mr. Lawyer went over my head and pulled a story off the air. It was the last straw after a happy six years at CKY.

I have many fond memories of Winnipeg. My two youngest children, Lee-Anne and Ryan, were born at St. Boniface Hospital. We were settled and happy and I considered remaining in the city and starting my own media business. But there were other concerns. My father was in poor health and I wanted my children to experience life on the east coast. To make matters easier for me, I had a standing job offer from Radio Station CHNS in Halifax. So in 1978 I came home. This time to stay.

8

Halifax, 1978

CHNS, University of King's College and CRXL

I was back in Halifax, the city I loved, but I felt like a fish out of water. I was close to my parents, renewed many old friendships, visited familiar places that were special to me yet I felt very much out of place. People from away say you need time to settle into the Maritime lifestyle and maybe you do, because I found my first year back in Nova Scotia happy but unsettling. Part of it was the hectic pace I set for myself.

I had three jobs and running from one to the other was nerve-wracking. Besides writing and delivering two radio commentaries each day on CHNS, I was also teaching at the University of King's College. It was the first year for the School of Journalism and I instructed students on news reading as well as on writing for radio. Then I would dash off to the other end of the city to teach in a continuing education program, which operated the student radio station, CRXL.

My day started before 7 a.m. at CHNS, then off to King's and on to the World Trade Centre and CRXL. I loved teaching and enjoyed the students, but – excuse the pun – I wasn't really anchored anywhere. The radio work was solitary and the teaching jobs only part-time. Maybe I was missing the responsibility of management and the team camaraderie of television.

As far as commentaries went, the world was my oyster. I had total control over the subject matter and editorial point of view, and in 1978 there was a vast array of issues to write about.

I'd arrived back in Halifax in the last months of Gerald Regan's Liberal government and at the conclusion of the Mercator controversy. The Mercator was a cruise ship the Regan regime wanted to operate. The idea was simple, or so it seemed to the backers. In a province almost completely surrounded by water, why not have our own a cruise ship to carry visitors from southern ports to beautiful Nova Scotia? Cruises could run out of Halifax and the profits could go to the government.

The controversy that arose plowed through the waters of the Regan government, stopping the plan dead in its tracks. The seafarers were upset over the hiring of a foreign crew, the Opposition was upset over the cost, complaints from taxpayers rained down on the government and eventually the Mercator was another unfulfilled dream dashed on the rocks of political controversy. It wasn't the only ship tied up on the Halifax waterfront in the late '70s with millions of taxpayers' dollars in its hulls.

Commentary, September 1978: The Seas of Controversy

Two ships, both unneeded and unwanted, sit and wait in Nova Scotia. One of the first challenges facing the new Buchanan government is what to do with the *Mercator*. The answer seems to be sell the cruise ship that hasn't cruised in quite a while. Looking for a buyer is one thing but finding someone interested in laying the cash on the line is quite another.

The new worry with the *Mercator* is the fact that even a ship tied up at dockside needs to be lavished with money to keep it seaworthy. The *Mercator* is going to require additional money for upkeep and seaworthiness. If the ship isn't sold soon, the province will have to lay out additional cash to keep it fit.

The second ship – the world's fastest and finest hydrofoil – is the *Bras d'Or*. The multi-million-dollar experiment, the pride of the navy, now roosts like a wounded seagull on the Halifax waterfront. The Department of Defense has even been talking to museums and the Canadian National Exhibition. Anyone can – according to a spokesman for the Defense Department – get a real deal. The Bras d'Or costs somewhere in the vicinity of $53 million.

Please note: while the *Bras d'Or* sits in idleness for seven years, the United States Navy steps up its hydrofoil program.

Please note: the cruise ship *Europa* arrives in Halifax this morning. She has been cruising around Nova Scotia carrying six hundred German tourists.

The only thing carried on the *Bras d'Or* and the *Mercator* is a heavy debt. Two good ideas that went awry: ideas for the future whose past is still costing us.

The 1978 Election

It wasn't shipping but power rates that brought down the Regan government. Voters were stung by higher electric costs and they were grumpy. The *Mercator* controversy was seen as a waste of money. It wasn't the deciding factor but it didn't help things either.

I hosted the Nova Scotia election coverage on CHNS as well as a candidates' debate during the election campaign which pitted Regan's Liberals against John Buchanan's Conservatives. One of the novice Conservative candidates was a young Dartmouth lawyer, Tom McInnis, who was trying to unseat veteran Liberal A. Garnet Brown. No question, Brown was a Liberal powerhouse. He had been highways minister in the Regan government and had money to mount a strong campaign.

Brown wasn't in the studio in person for some reason, but was on the speaker phone. I was sitting with half a dozen candidates at a round table in the big radio studio at CHNS, where they used to do radio drama. McInnis was seated next to me. It was his first campaign and he was so nervous when the gruff Garnet Brown started attacking him, he visibly trembled to such an extent I became concerned that he was going to completely lose his composure. He didn't. In fact, he held his own in the debate and went on to win the election. Tom McInnis went further, to become Attorney General of Nova Scotia and a polished politician. In other words, he got over the jitters.

The Post Office Gets Crowned

Looking back at the '70s, it's surprising now how often the post office was in the news and how controversial the Canadian postal service was in those days. There were continuing complaints over the price of stamps. When stamps increased to seventeen cents there was grumbling across the land. Dissatisfaction with the post office paved the way for the flourishing of private courier companies and the federal government finally turned the post office into a Crown corporation. That fixed it, didn't it? Today's postal stamps don't have a price on them. A stamp now costs fifty-six cents but that will probably increase by the time you read this.

Lots of Complaints

As a nation we were worn down by the same old situations. We complained and complained and nothing really changed. It led to a certain attitude of surrender and that's one reason why we have become so passive about our politics and our leadership.

In the 1970s we complained more than we do today. Complaints about the economy were continuous. A family home was $20,000 or $25,000. The price paid for an original and very rare Gutenberg Bible that went up for auction in New York was $2 million. In 1978 it was the highest price ever paid for a printed book. Today $2 million wouldn't buy you much of a condo in New York City and rare books and paintings sell for $100 million or more. Prices were lower but inflation was higher. There were wage and price controls that really controlled wages but not so much prices. Remember Beryl Plumtree and the Food Prices Review Board?

Back in the days of Federal Minister of Agriculture Eugene Whalen, Beryl Plumtree took on the task of having the government pay for all surplus eggs and butter from the dairy farmers. Whalen agreed to assume responsibility for any future surplus and to protect farmers against other countries dumping their product on our markets. This led eventually to the development of NAFTA, the FTA, GATT and WTO.

Wage and price controls were actually Bob Stanfield's idea. Pierre Trudeau vigorously campaigned against the concept in the federal election, criss-crossing the country and rejecting the concept at every stop. Most Canadians agreed with him. Who wanted their wages controlled by government? Trudeau won, then turned around and implemented the very program he campaigned against. It's a Liberal trait. Jean Chrétien did the same thing. He campaigned against the GST then implemented it. Dalton McGinty campaigned against raising taxes then raised them. Did those broken promises hurt these men politically? Not a bit.

If we could only remember from one election to the next that we'd been lied to, we'd have at least a more honest government, if no more capable.

Compared to the problems we face today the '70s were rather tranquil times. Today our economic problems are tied into and overshadowed by environmental issues that have dire consequences for all of us. With a threatened planet this is hardly the time for more passivism about government policies. The Alberta tar sands continue to be the world's biggest environmental disaster, spewing billions of gallons of toxic debris into our atmosphere, yet the federal and Alberta governments act as if there isn't a problem. Corporate profits are competing with saving the planet. It is surprising that money is winning.

We're passive on foreign policy too. There is not much reporting concerning the ongoing butchery in Darfur. It's much the same as the genocide in Rwanda. The world keeps looking away. In a few years we'll be asking how all this could have happened.

On the world stage in '78 Central America was in turmoil. In Nicaragua, the Sandinista guerrillas mounted a campaign to rid the country of the murderous regime of Anastasio Somoza. The United States was, of course, on the wrong side, assisting the dictator in his bid to hold on to power. The Western media always described the rebellion as a leftist movement, as if that was justification for crushing it. What was really happening in Nicaragua was a rebellion of the poor and oppressed who had no share in the country's wealth. What limited wealth there was went to foreign corporations, the dictator Somoza and his cronies. Somoza ruled with an iron hand. Opposition was brutally stifled and those who defied the dictator disappeared in the night. Eventually, after great suffering, the Sandinistas were successful and Somoza snuck away in the middle of the night, taking his dead father with him for fear the corpse would be desecrated.

The story of Nicaragua is but one example of how poor people are ground down and when they can't take it anymore, they revolt. If they are opposing something American, say U.S. foreign policy or U.S. industrial or corporate domination, then the story is formed and molded in Washington that these people are part of a sinister, nefarious uprising carried out by Communists/rebels/insurgents/bad people. Unfortunately, many of us in the media and many of those in government believed the U.S. spin in the '70s and '80s.

My experience with United States governmental policy is that it never admits it is wrong, no matter how horribly miscalculated, selfish and hurtful its policies actually are to people in other parts of the world – people who are usually poor but live in a land of great resources wanted by the United States or its rich corporations.

To a certain extent the public has moved ahead of the U.S. media. The media still buys the U.S. point of view but it is less trusted today. Now the news is spewed out twenty-four hours a day on all news networks that do little more than skim the surface of any issue. However, the world is changing. The United States is losing its pre-eminent global position. The prestige it once held has been diminished by such disasters as Vietnam and Iraq. As well, keeping people in jail without trial, whisking people away to secret prisons in foreign lands, torture and murder have all played a part in the decline of the United States.

* * *

At CHNS I wrote commentaries for the 8 a.m. news and 5 p.m. news. I dug into everything, poked fun at everything, flattered or criticized everyone and touched some very touchy subjects, such as Maritime work habits.

Commentary, February 1979: Working Hard or Hardly Working

There was a lot of reaction to last week's report which found workers in the have-not areas of Canada were not as productive as those in richer regions. The report struck at the heart of the Maritime image. It confirmed what many Canadians believe about us: quaint and slow, Peggy's Cove and foggy harbours.

Because the report came close to the truth, it had to be condemned and, of course, it was, by business leaders, union leaders and the Maritime media. Examples were given where companies in this part of Canada outperformed others and business leaders claimed it wasn't the worker at fault; it was the equipment or the management, anything – but certainly not the worker.

Maybe you buy that. I don't. Workers do lack drive in this part of Canada and, instead of denying it, we should look at the reason why. This is not meant to be a condemnation of every social program established in the last twenty years to assist workers but when government does well, it can have bad repercussions. Giving by government leads to taking it for granted.

Nova Scotia is looked upon as being a nice place, filled with the wrinkled faces of fishermen. Instead of looking at a study that might have much validity, we simply refuse to look, terribly afraid we might see the truth. The problem with this attitude is it won't help make Maritimers become more interested in what they do. It won't make our businesses more productive, it won't give us a little more drive. Trouble is, with our heads firmly buried in the sand, it's difficult to see the truth.

* * *

Needless to say, that was not a big hit with the Board of Trade. But what couldn't be denied was that every time a critical assessment of our productivity appeared concerning our fisheries, forestry, offshore oil or labour force, a great swarm of deniers and naysayers suddenly appeared to contradict any thoughtful analysis that faulted productivity. That reaction wasn't particularly helpful. Our economic development might have been enhanced if we had really considered such findings rather than blindly rejected them.

The *Halifax Herald* had always been a backer of the status quo, particularly in the 1970s, pandering to the old Bluenose establishment. Such establishment media outlets were hardly ready for a guy like Pierre Trudeau, who was making noises about repatriating the constitution. People were suspicious about his intentions. After all, he was different and we didn't like different. There was already considerable tension between French and English Canada, so all that was needed was a match to fan the flames. When rumours spread that Trudeau was going to turn Canada into a republic, well – what did that mean? Was the Queen getting the axe?

The reaction was so forceful and vocal the government was caught off guard by the ensuing eruption. It issued public assurances it had no intention of replacing the monarch. The old establishment newspapers were relieved. I took another tack because I felt the government had fallen on its sword and instead of standing up to its critics, it seemed to be putting the entire idea of repatriation on the back burner.

Commentary, August 1978: Long Live The Queen

The Monarchy is safe. There is no danger. The Queen has many protectors, particularly in this part of the nation but in other parts of Canada as well. The Royal Family will continue and the Queen will hold her status. Her defenders are now jumping out of the woodwork faster than lemmings jump into the sea. It's good to see this reaction in some ways; it demonstrates that cold Canadians can get worked into a lather. It shows there are still emotional sparks to light the fuse. The pro-monarchists rise up like a tidal wave ready to do battle with any and all. Who would dare even suggest that perhaps it's time for a review? The Queen is safe.

But it's not all positive. The emotional onslaught has dashed any hope for a new constitution for Canada. It even destroyed the prospect of a healthy public discussion on the matter. And I can't help but wonder and wish that Canadians could get as worked up over other concerns: the lack of jobs, the growth of government, the cost of food and power, plus the grinding poverty faced by some.

As a society we're content to let social injustices pass. We permit senior citizens to eat dog food because fixed incomes keep them below the poverty line. Where's the emotionalism about them? Where are all these royal defenders? If only they could show as much concern on other issues. They will contribute nothing to redesigning a constitution for Canada but they will kill any attempt by others to do so. They will deny the nation progress because they fear the long-time symbol of the British throne will not survive. They don't even have faith in each other or what they stand for.

The Queen is safe, and if her defenders don't dash the ship of state in their emotional spree, we might even have intelligent discussion resulting in a new constitution and the continuation of the Queen. The Queen will survive. The question is, will Canada?

* * *

Sounds rather dramatic today, but in the 1970s Canada was rubbed raw by the impact of the many social changes of the '60s, among them the rising voice of Quebec nationalism. We did finally get a new constitution. It was Trudeau's greatest achievement. The monarchy survived too. But I wouldn't bet it will last more than a few decades after the death of Queen Elizabeth. Of course, I've been wrong before.

After a year at CHNS I had finally settled into life in Nova Scotia. However, the radio station wanted more of my time and more of me on the air. I was suddenly informed I was to read the 7:00 and 8:00 a.m. major morning newscasts as an added responsibility while still retaining the two daily commentaries. That was a far cry from my original agreement with the station. It also meant being in the station even earlier as I now had to prepare the news, edit the copy and rewrite wire copy as well as writing my commentaries. It was doable but it wasn't the deal I had made with the station a year earlier when I was hired. However, I was a company man and I tried to be a good employee.

I plodded along for a few weeks until one day Dick Prat and I went to lunch together. By then Dick was the news director at CJCH Television. CHUM Toronto planned to amalgamate the Halifax, Moncton and Sydney stations into one system. Dick had big plans too for the television newsroom. He was progressive and the type of guy to get his own way when he wanted something. What he wanted was to build a top-flight news-gathering operation. His newsroom was one of the first in the country to switch from film to video tape. It would also be one of the very first to use computers. Dick wanted to establish a full-time documentary unit. He asked me if I would consider leaving CHNS and heading up the new documentary venture. Without hesitation I agreed. I'd done some documentary work in Calgary and Winnipeg and I found it rewarding.

So I made another career move back to CJCH, soon to become ATV, where I would remain for almost a decade and where great adventures awaited me.

9

Halifax and On the Road, 1980s

The Team

Dick Prat had put together a great documentary team. Chuck Stewart was the field producer. Chuck had plenty of experience, starting his career as a photographer. Barry Bramhill was our cameraman. He was a good shooter and a real character. Barry would often show up for a three-day road trip with a bag of tomatoes, a loaf of bread and a jar of mayonnaise, explaining he had spent his food per diem. Don Pepin was our young audio operator. He was a quick study who would become a producer and eventually join CBC sports. I picked the stories, did the hosting, writing and interviews. We were a solid team and we worked hard, were diligent in our efforts and had plenty of good times too.

Bathurst Home Furnishings

One of our first field trips was to Bathurst, New Brunswick. The subject was police strikes in the Maritimes and Bathurst was one of the communities hit by such a disruptive labour stoppage. We were naturally all excited about our documentary unit and after work we were ready to let off steam. We checked into a local motel, discussed the day's events and looked at some of the tape we had shot.

After a few beers, our creative juices were apparently rekindled. Maybe it was the beer or maybe it was just the warm spring night and the fact we had the entire motel to ourselves. Maybe we were going through some form of second childhood. Who really knows why grown men do silly things. Whatever the reason, sometime during the evening and over many laughs, we decided to make a commercial just for a lark. We lugged the furniture out of our motel rooms to the parking lot: tables, chairs and chesterfields. We set up an outdoor living room and then set up the camera.

We made an unrehearsed, unscripted commercial right on the spot for Bathurst Home Furnishings. We didn't know if there was such a company and I'm sure they wouldn't want to use our talents on the air. Things are a bit hazy concerning the commercial, but I believe we did many different takes and took turns before the camera as the pitchman, selling Bathurst Home Furnishings, while, of course, holding a beer. On some takes there were two of us selling the benefits of furniture at deep discount "hiccup" prices. It was hilarious, or at least we thought it was at the time. Miraculously, no one called the police, which was a good thing! Their police strike had been settled by then.

The team, the travel, the challenge of producing first-rate news documentaries made it a dream job. What I didn't dream was that fate had other plans in store for me.

Three months after we started the documentary unit, the station's 6 p.m. anchor, Terry Glecoff, resigned to take a job in Calgary. A number of staff people were designated to read the news while a permanent replacement was found. I was one of those picked to fill in for a few nights. By that time I'd done years of commentaries in Winnipeg and I was comfortable enough in front of the camera. I wasn't nervous either because I didn't want the anchor job. It was too restrictive to be wired into an anchor desk, with some dude in the control room talking into your earpiece, telling you while you're reading that the next story isn't ready, so drop it and move to the crime report. I detested the daily ritual of makeup, and after twenty years of anchoring that feeling has remained.

More importantly, I didn't like life in a fishbowl. I had experience enough with public recognition in western Canada. When my nightly commentaries started in Winnipeg, the first person to accost me in public was an excitable, talkative Ukrainian lady in a supermarket. She gushed as if I were a rock star. My wife thought it was hilarious, especially when I turned crimson. I realized that if I stayed on the anchor desk I was going to have to accept certain things, such as losing my privacy. I enjoyed the anonymity of documentary work, where I might eventually become a known face in the Maritimes but it would take considerably more time.

Dick called me into his office one morning. Not the type of man to beat around the bush, Dick put his question point blank: Did I want the anchor job full-time?

"No thanks," I replied.

Dick suspected my answer but, of course, he had a very strong card to play next.

"There's more money in it," he said.

It wasn't just a raise but a substantial readjustment in my salary, enough to give me pause to think. We had purchased a nice home in the Nantucket section of Dartmouth. The pay hike was more money than we made on the sale of our Winnipeg home. I had three children to consider. In addition, there was no question that Nova Scotia was a far more expensive place to live than Manitoba.

I didn't particularly care for anchoring but I had a family to think about and frankly, I was torn. Besides money, there were other benefits to anchoring, none more important than the possibility of travel and the opportunity to do major stories in other lands. It was also an honour to head up a progressive news team and there was no question that Dick was aiming to build the best team possible.

We finally reached a compromise. We agreed that the best course was for me to try the anchor job for a few weeks to see if I could adjust. I became embroiled in the job and weeks turned into months and autumn arrived and in television land that's promo time, when the big push is on for the fall programming. I was promoted as the face of the ATV *Evening News* and I settled in for the long run as a television anchorman.

The Transition to ATV

The following months saw many changes in the newsroom. Dick brought Dave Wright over from CJ radio to do a magazine-type lead-in show to the news. The show was to run from 5:30 to 6:00 p.m. The idea was to take Dave's show outside the station as much as possible. We had discussions on how to handle this new concept and what it should look like. I suggested we call it *Dave Wright's Video Notebook*, and Dick finally chose *The Notebook with Dave Wright*. After a season or two the show was extended to an hour and turned into Live at 5. By that time CJCH Television had become ATV.

Of course, most great ideas aren't born without mistakes and a lot of fine-tuning. During the early weeks of *Live at 5* and the Evening News there were initial errors and readjustments. Moving us into a ninety-minute news block meant doing away with the local newscasts in Moncton and Sydney and amalgamating all efforts into one regional broadcast covering the news from all three Maritime Provinces out of Halifax. There were plenty of dire predictions that we would go down in flames. Critics said viewers in other communities wouldn't stand for their local news coming from Halifax. They would change channels. It will never work. Who wants to see our news coming from Halifax? We had a cloud hanging over our heads from the start.

There were still vital questions to be answered. Chief among them was what the new Maritime amalgamated newscast was going to look like on air. With Don Pepin looking after the control room and much of the technical responsibilities, Dick Prat drew up a plan for transferring the local anchors from Moncton and Sydney to Halifax. They were, after all, recognizable faces in their own communities. Dick's concept was the local anchors would have mini anchor desks in the Halifax newsroom located somewhere behind me. When there was a story from Cape Breton I'd read a lead line and throw it to Bill Jessome. He'd read the rest of the introduction and throw it to the Cape Breton reporter covering the story. Eric Sorensen would do the same for New Brunswick stories.

Sounds convoluted, doesn't it? Believe me, it was. It only took about two nightly newscasts to see the system was awkward and cumbersome. There were simply too many anchors. Eric returned to New Brunswick to head our bureau there. Bill Jessome joined the Halifax reporting staff, where he did hard news and features for many years.

Dave Wright

Dave Wright and I were colleagues for almost ten years. We didn't socialize outside of work, probably because we were quite different in our likes and dislikes. I enjoyed food and fine wine and he liked cards and blackjack. On the air we were different too. I came across as the serious voice of the news, while Wright was light and airy, which suited the more relaxed tone of his show. Off camera we were in contrast to our on-air demeanour. I was apt to be the more relaxed one and Dave was certainly more driven. That's television, isn't it?

In the early days of *Live at 5*, Dave and I went through a period of adjustment. I felt he was encroaching into the news world, where he would take a breaking story and carve it up for *Live at 5*, before it ever got on the *Evening News*. It may sound silly, but protecting our own program is part of the business. I've seen it happen at the network level where I've requested video from CTV News and the producer said, "Fine, but don't give it to *Canada AM*" (CTV's morning show).

After some early friction, Dave and I smoothed things out and basically had a good working relationship. We still bickered occasionally over stories because we were both aggressive and competitive. But for most of our years working together, we got along.

We also shared some funny experiences. Early on, Dick Prat took Dave and me to lunch at a high-end Halifax restaurant. It was the first time I ever had a meal with Dave Wright and I was shocked when he ordered his steak burnt. Not just well done but burnt to a crisp. The chef thought it was funny too. He came right out of the kitchen wanting to see the guy who purposely desired to destroy one of his prime cuts. The chef was a big guy, wearing the traditional white hat that made him appear seven feet tall. I snuck a look at his hands, just to make sure he wasn't holding a cleaver.

In Cape Breton one time we were doing promos atop city hall in Sydney. It's one of the tallest buildings in town that gave the camera a panoramic view. The cameraman kept telling us to step back, step back. Now, we were several stories above the ground with no railing on the roof, and Dave and I were getting more uncomfortable with every centimetre we crept closer to the edge. One more step, we reasoned, and they'd be looking for two new hosts at ATV.

Although our tastes were different Dave and I had some common interests. We were both movie buffs and we were both competitive. He was a great showman and we both benefitted from a great technical team behind us.

As for those dire predictions of viewers turning us off in droves? Well, it simply didn't happen. In fact, more viewers tuned in. In the first months we saw we had a formula for success. Between Live at 5 and the ATV Evening News we formed a ninety-minute block of air time that had extremely high ratings. It's a formula that is still working today.

The Thornhill Affair

The stories, of course, make the newscast. We covered the usual array of stories in the ATV newsroom. There is always murder and mayhem in city life and what newsroom hasn't covered the dotty woman with twenty-five cats. There were strikes and walkouts, news conferences, eccentrics with theories and people claiming they've been kidnapped by aliens. There was investigative work too. Reporter Blain Henshaw dove into a story concerning Buchanan cabinet minister Roland Thornhill. With the help of tycoon Harry Steel, his high-powered brother-in-law, Thornhill paid off a deep personal debt. That wouldn't have been a story except Thornhill paid the chartered banks only twenty-five cents on the dollar and they called things even. Since when did the banks let you pay off your loan at twenty-five cents on the dollar?

There was a cry that Thornhill had received special treatment because he was Nova Scotia's Minister of Economic Development. In other words, a man the banks needed to know if they wanted lucrative government business. When there is a controversy involving the chartered banks, don't expect much cooperation. The banks love you when you're buying money from them, but when you ask questions they'd rather not answer, the stone wall goes up, shielding the top executives. All inquiries are suddenly handled by their public relations people who, after all, are supposed to know how to handle the media.

The Thornhill story also involved the Superintendent of Insurance, the main regulator for the insurance industry. Henshaw did a lot of digging and the more he dug, the more the story smelled. We both liked Rollie Thornhill personally and there was no malice on our part. It wasn't him we were after anyway, but the privilege system itself that puts ordinary citizens under the gun for failure to pay and gives powerful cabinet ministers a big break by writing off most of their personal debts without bankruptcy.

The Thornhill story got a lot of airplay but eventually petered out. Thornhill remained in office, the bankers retained their shield of silence and the insurance industry remained as it was. Those without connections and political power still had to pay what they owed without benefit of a break or face the stigma of bankruptcy. We gave the system a good airing but we didn't change anything. The system of privilege existed in Nova Scotia before the days of Joe Howe and still does today. Rollie Thornhill simply exemplified it.

Foreign Lands

The hoped-for travel aspect of anchoring came true. The anchor is the principal reporter for the company and as such covers the big stories outside the Maritimes. Dick Prat believed in sending his anchor people out of the studio and into the field. When the Berlin Wall came down, Dave Wright was there. When George Hees commemorated Canadian war graves in Hong Kong, I was there. Wright was in Poland and England; I did stand-ups in

Rangoon, in the harbour of Singapore and in downtown Tokyo.

Besides significant travel I also had an opportunity to keep a hand in documentaries. The documentary unit fell by the wayside when I went into the anchor job. Not because I left, but I think the company found the cost rather prohibitive, having four guys constantly on the road. Still, we had substantial resources and if Dick agreed with my idea, I'd be given time away from the anchor desk to go into the field for some in-depth documentary work.

Along with cameraman Wayne Clark and producer Don Pepin, we did a documentary on unemployment in Cape Breton entitled *Being Poor*. It was a personal look at the impact on families suffering from long-term unemployment caused by layoffs in the coal mines and the steel mill. On one occasion I was interviewing a laid-off steel worker who was optimistic he would soon be called on the job. "And how long have you been laid off?" I asked, expecting, due to his optimism, that he'd answer a month or two.

"Two years," he replied. He'd run out of benefits but not hope and the idea of relocating was something he wouldn't consider. Many Cape Bretoners didn't want to think about it either. Like Newfoundlanders, Cape Bretoners are homebodies. Family ties are strong and so is their sense of belonging. That's changed somewhat in recent times because of the wealth and employment in Alberta. But even so, while many go, most eventually return home.

Being Poor won us a national Can Pro award in 1982 as best news documentary and as broadcasters the world over do when they win an award, we happily reported the fact.

Roger Smith

There were many controversial stories at ATV in the 1980s. One concerned former Dartmouth police chief Roger Smith. Smith claimed an ATV report by Pat Ryan raised suspicions about his professional and personal conduct by reporting on a private loan Smith had received from a businessman. My involvement in the story was limited to reading the introduction to Ryan's report but I was named as one of the defendants.

When Smith sued for libel and defamation, ATV entered a not guilty plea and after weeks of meetings and trial preparation, we went to court. Of course, this was big news to the other media, who relished the chance to play up our situation. It was a jury trial at the Halifax Law Courts and on the first day of proceedings I knew we were in trouble. Pat Ryan took the stand first and he was too combative, giving the impression we were uncaring about the feelings of the Smith family. We weren't uncaring and I don't think Pat meant to come across as belligerent and feisty, but he did and you could read the agitation on the faces of the jury. We never recovered.

There was a photograph of me in the Halifax *Daily News*, taken when I was leaving the courtroom. I had my raincoat over my arm like George Raft in an old gangster movie. The caption read, "Defendant Graham leaving court." I looked like a convicted mafia don or one of those white-collar criminals that abscond with millions. Oh well, as they say, what's good for the goose is good for the gander.

We lost the case, of course, but the fine was never made public, although it should have been. No company under any such circumstances should be able to hide under a last-minute deal, but we did when it was obvious we were going to lose. The lawyers huddled and the deal was struck, meaning we paid an acceptable amount in a private negotiation and the jury was dismissed without reaching a verdict.

ATV would never reveal what it had to pay Roger Smith, not even to us. Nor did they reveal how much the entire case cost them, which wasn't any of our business anyway. Defamation cases were coming into vogue in the '80s and they were putting a chill over investigative reporting. It was, and unfortunately still is, a very easy excuse used by many lazy reporters for not digging.

The Trudeau Pirouette

One of my favourite stories of Pierre Trudeau was the night in Ottawa when he said goodbye to the Liberal Party. It was a night to remember and a lesson to be learned by anyone operating a video camera. Remember the first rule of covering a news story. Deciding when to turn your camera on and off is a critical editorial decision. As Yogi Berra said, "It ain't over till it's over," and Trudeau liked surprises.

It was the night before a new leader (Jean Chrétien) was chosen. Amid a rousing ovation, Trudeau finished his farewell speech, bowed to thousands of cheering delegates and left the stage behind the curtains. Only one cameraman with Radio Canada, the French CBC, kept rolling. He either had a hunch or he was lucky because Trudeau suddenly reappeared, did a pirouette before the cheering throng and disappeared again. That twirl said more about the man than the speech had. There was mayhem among television producers and camera people, trying to get a copy of the Trudeau twirl. It was great video. Of a dozen cameras, one had kept rolling to capture the swirl.

Richard Hatfield

What swirled around New Brunswick premier Richard Hatfield in the 1980s was a different kind of dance. The high-flying Hatfield was often criticized for his many trips to New York. ATV reporter Andy LeBlanc went through eighteen months worth of the premier's travel expenses. What he found was that the premier was billing both the Conservative party and the province of New Brunswick for the same expense.

In March of 1986, LeBlanc ran the story of the double billing with video that included the actual travel expenses. A sharp-eyed viewer called the station. He had seen something we had missed. One of the expenses was for a bookstore called Androgynous Books. We had the name but not the address of the store or even what city it was in. LeBlanc and I spent most of an afternoon phoning city directories around North America looking for it, which we eventually located in Montreal. It was a store specializing in homosexual literature. It was difficult to see how that could be a taxpayer expense. However, the story never got to air as the Conservatives convinced Andy this was a party and a personal affair.

Hatfield was often shielded, even by us, but it didn't curtail his meandering ways. There was the marijuana story. Premier Hatfield was charged after the Mounties discovered a bag of weed in his suitcase. He was boarding an aircraft taking dignitaries and the media to greet Queen Elizabeth during her 1984 Canadian visit. Hatfield denied the weed was his and hired a high-powered lawyer, who at the trial pointed the finger at ATV reporter Pat Ryan (the same reporter who wrote the Roger Smith story). Ryan had been transferred to Fredericton with ATV and he was pointed to as the probable culprit who planted the dope in the premier's suitcase. The accusation from Hatfield's lawyers was that Ryan was trying to make a news story and embarrass the premier because the media was out to "get" Hatfield. It was so incredibly far-fetched no one believed it but that didn't matter, and it cast some doubt on the Crown's case. Hatfield, as expected, got off and Ryan had his reputation besmirched.

After that incident, Hatfield was accused of snorting cocaine with university students. Yes! Why stop at marijuana when you have coke too. There were enough witnesses to make the story credible and that story we did run in the mid-'80s. One of the students told of seeing the premier with white power caked on his nose. When a premier hooks up with a group of young people and spends the evening doing drugs, it's a big story. It was our lead on the 6 p.m. news. As I read the words about white powder on the premier's nose I wondered how the thousands of New Brunswick viewers would react. Some were horrified, but many weren't. They accepted the premier's peccadilloes and that was the end of that.

By that time, Hatfield was already near the end of a long political career that wasn't without accomplishments. He had modernized one of the worst highway systems in the country. He had made thousands of Acadians equal partners in public life by recognizing French as one of New Brunswick's official languages. He was seen as a senior Canadian statesman. Had he been more courageous he would have stood up, admitted the weed was his and accepted the misdemeanour fine. I would have had more respect for the man.

The Hash Brownie Meeting

While on the subject of cannabis, an event occurred about this time that had absolutely no political consequences but is one of the lingering stories still told by the older staff. The story involves an ATV news meeting.

From time to time it is necessary for news directors to hold departmental meetings. There are always projects underway, new events to cover, new subjects and procedures to introduce and regulations to tighten or modify. With a large staff on different shifts it is difficult to get everybody together. When the night shift arrives in late afternoon there is panic to get the 6 p.m. news on the air and the dayshift is busy with show prep. At ATV we often had working dinners where the company would bring in pizza and soft drinks, but when Dick was severely over budget he scheduled meetings at 8:00 at night. That gave the day shift time to grab a bite, saving on food costs.

It just so happened on one particular night when such an evening meeting was scheduled, a new Wendy's restaurant was holding its official opening in the Spryfield area of Halifax. The entire news staff had received invitations to a wine and cheese party to launch the hamburger franchise. Since we had an hour to kill, several of us jumped in a car to grab a glass of wine and have a little breather before the meeting.

Erstwhile cameraman/producer Barry Bramhill happened to have a tray of hash brownies which he passed around the car on our way to the wine and cheese. Everybody but the driver had one or two of these brownies. I had never eaten hash brownies but they tasted fine and didn't seem to bother me. At the reception I didn't think anything more about them. We had a couple of glasses of wine, met the national president of Wendy's and went back for the news meeting. It was on the way back to the station that the passengers in the crowded car, who had been boisterous on the way to the reception, suddenly fell very silent. We became contemplative, meditative and, well – stoned.

It was the most peculiar news meeting in the history of television journalism. These gatherings are usually noisy affairs. Not this one. Dick talked and we sat at our desks as mute as manikins. At one point, I looked around at one of my colleagues who were staring straight ahead. His eyes were as big as saucers and totally vacant. Whatever planet he was on, it was definitely far away from Mother Earth.

Dick finished his talk and waited for our reaction. We were always vocal and he expected our comments, questions and criticism. There weren't any. You could hear a pin drop. He was talking to a room full of zombies. As I recall, that was the last 8 p.m. news meeting at ATV.

ASN

Two significant things happened at ATV during the 1980s. For the company, one was a happy occasion and one was not.

The Canadian Radio, Television and Telecommunications Commission wanted to find ways to bring broadcast signals to people in remote parts of Canada. It called for proposals from broadcasters to reach underserved and remote areas. CHUM came up with the idea for a satellite service. It prepared its presentation, took it to the commission and won approval to establish ASN.

It was a victory for the company, but it was something else too. ASN was also seen as a way of preventing another broadcasting company from applying for a television license in the rapidly growing Halifax-Dartmouth market. If successful, the new service would have its own newsroom and its own anchors. (It doesn't today. It just simulcasts the CTV service.) ASN was successful amid great celebration. A mini-newsroom was built along the back wall of ATV so we had a newsroom within a newsroom.

We were an impressive operation by then. We had top-level U.S. television news consultants out of Washington, D.C. We were still leading the ratings and cutting new ground technically. We had a fully computerized newsroom and ASN was a satellite system that carried its signal far and wide to remote parts of Canada. If it wasn't the big time, it looked and felt like the big time, and broadcasters came to have a look at our facilities and study our success. The only problem was, people were generally dissatisfied and unhappy.

The Union

I've run both radio and television newsrooms and I know it is impossible to keep a large staff happy at all times. News people are usually highly creative people, the type of people who need constant stimulation and challenges. It only takes one or two agitators to cause a great deal of unrest. Somewhere along the line in those heady days of the mid-'80s, amidst all our success, the staff at ATV no longer felt a sense of purpose. You suddenly heard the word "union" muttered along the corridors and in the coffee shop.

The drive to unionize the newsroom fractured the staff and further deteriorated relations between staff and management. People became testy and the happy, smiling on-air demeanour disappeared the moment the cameras were off. As an anchor, I was under contract to the company and the union drive by ACTRA didn't involve me directly. It certainly did indirectly. In television nobody works in a vacuum. When your colleagues are caught up in animosity it affects you. Strain enveloped the workplace.

When negotiations stalled, the union brought in some high-profile people to lend support. When I arrived for work one morning, the first person to greet me was Ed Asner (Lou Grant on the *Mary Tyler Moore Show*). He was standing in the parking lot with the ACTRA rep. I was introduced as the station's news anchor. Asner shook my hand then ran his hand over the lapel of my top coat. "Nice coat," he said. The insinuation was clear. I was well-paid and thus could afford better clothing than some of my colleagues.

What he didn't realize was that I had come through the ranks and was no different from my colleagues.

To a great degree the union drive involved the salaries of women, who were paid less than men. I swore then if I was ever again a news director the pay scale between men and woman would be equal. That's exactly what I took steps to bring about a few years later at MITV.

After several hectic months there was finally a settlement at ATV and people deservedly received higher salaries. But they lost something too. The work environment was never the same. The hostility had festered too long and flowered more openly in future union negotiations.

Of course, ATV was vulnerable to a union. The station had grown, the company was extremely prosperous, and the workers felt they weren't getting enough of the pie. Changing social values reflected a different work ethic and an erosion of company loyalty. Women made up much of the workforce. They were paid less and contributed as much or more than men. Certainly some of our finest reporters were hard-working women who sought more equality and who could blame them?

Letters – We Got Letters

By the time the union was established at ATV, I had been anchoring the news for several years. Thousands of Maritimers let me into their living rooms every night. Some of them wrote me glowing letters. Some thought they were my mother and told me not to wear a certain tie or to get a hair cut or that Laura Lee Langley was the best weather person in the world but why does she wear that awful blouse, as if I personally picked out Laura Lee's clothing. Little boys wrote asking me how much money I made and was it easy to be a television anchor.

For a year, I received a series of strange letters from a woman in Cape Breton. They were voluminous stream-of-consciousness epistles, harmless at first, describing her life with her husband and daughter. As the months unfolded her letters became more familiar and personal and lustful. I didn't respond, believing she would eventually tire of the one-way correspondence. Finally, she was having sexual fantasies in which I had stepped out of the television set to seduce her. During the last months of her correspondence, she enclosed her photograph. She was middle-aged and not only was she in love with me but loved making love to me. She believed I was there with her. It wasn't like the movie *Play Misty for Me*. I didn't feel in danger, just sorry for her. Her letters finally just stopped and I never heard from her again.

Another viewer informed Laura Lee Langley that he watched our program every night and when he closed one eye he could tell the side of my head was slowly being crushed by aliens. Wow!

By then, after years on air, I had accepted the recognition factor. There is no way around it – you're on television every night, your photo is in the newspapers, you give speeches, visit schools and host election coverages. But sometimes a strange experience will bring you back to reality very, very quickly.

One such experience happened to me during a lunch hour shopping trip to Scotia Square in downtown Halifax. I was looking for Christmas gifts. Walking along the indoor mall I noticed, in the reflections of the store windows, that I was being followed. Three people were behind me: a man, a woman and a young boy. When I entered a store they remained outside and resumed following me when I moved on. Finally, I stopped and turned to them. Timidly, the man approached and held out his hand.

"I watch every night, we all do. You're the best there is." Then he introduced his wife and his son. They were from the Eastern Shore and had come up to Halifax to shop for Christmas. We made some small talk about the weather and the Christmas season and the man reiterated that I was their favourite person on television. Again I thanked them and told them it was a very kind thing to say. We bid each other farewell and as I walked away I heard the man say to his son, "There, aren't you glad you finally got to meet Dave Wright?"

I laughed all the way back to the station. So did Dave Wright when I told him.

In the Field

During the last years at ATV, I had given up the writing and producing duties of the news completely. I still had control over editorial content on the Evening News but I was in the field almost every day. With excellent cameramen such as Al Eastman, Wayne Clark, Pat Kennedy, Jamie Munro, Dave Pike and many others, I travelled anywhere there was a story as long as I was back by 5:30 at the very latest. In the morning, my producer, Christine Holtroff, and I would go over the day's story prospects with the assignment desk. I would pick a story and then we'd be off to Amherst, Kentville or New Glasgow.

Once a cameraman and I drove to Country Harbour and filmed a story on the new gas pipeline coming ashore. We got it on air by the skin of our teeth and I rushed out of the editing suite and into the anchor chair, took a breath as the theme was playing and said, "Good Tuesday Evening."

Most days weren't that hectic. I'd read over the scripts that Christine had written, Dave Wright would wrap up another Live at 5 then I'd be on the air.

Arson

One of my very best pieces of work during the 1980s was a five-part series I did on arson investigations in Nova Scotia. The series was called *Ordeal by Fire* and, like all good reporters, it helps to be in the right place at the right time.

There had been disturbing indications that the Fire Marshal's office was making a lot of mistakes. They were charging innocent people with arson and getting convictions based on shoddy evidence. There were signs their investigative methods were faulty, their procedures poor and their science highly suspect. I did a lot of investigating, interviewing many highly trained technical people and engineers specializing in arson investigation. I travelled up and down the province talking to people who had gone through the hellish nightmare of facing criminal charges. One young man was accused of setting his car on fire but where was the proof? Then there was the businessman accused of setting his business ablaze. One experienced arson investigator, who was also a professional engineer, condemned much of the science used by the Fire Marshal's office and their hired experts.

The Fire Marshal's office defended their methods but wouldn't or couldn't respond to many of the charges. They were furious as the series ran episodically over five nights with one Nova Scotian after another telling their stories. The theme hit home as people realized it could happen to you or me or anyone. Any fire might be followed by the even more ghastly experience of facing criminal charges.

Two events happened following the series. The first was public and the second, which was more important, was not. The first was at a police forum in Cole Harbour where my series was praised publicly in front of hundreds of people by a high-ranking RCMP officer. Most people involved in the field of arson investigation knew there had been some miscarriages of justice. It was something known but not acknowledged.

The second event was done quietly, without fanfare or public announcement, as things are often done in Nova Scotia. The epidemic of arson cases which filled the courts based on the flimsy and erroneous evidence from the Fire Marshal's office and the insurance industry came to an end. The Attorney General issued instructions to the Crown Prosecutor's office that, except in cases of irrefutable evidence, no more cases of arson would go forward.

Arson investigator N.H. McFetridge wrote me a personal letter in January of 1986. He stated that the program was executed in the best tradition of investigative reporting. The innocent victims described the anguish and trauma they had endured without making the story maudlin. He also stated that too many TV journalists are tempted to attack the principal offender with accusatory questioning, whereas my program allowed him to condemn himself by his own words.

If there are better words of praise for one's work, I haven't heard them.

Strange Experiences

Life was busy, varied and interesting. When I got up in the morning I never knew where I'd be by lunchtime or who I'd be interviewing and what I'd be doing. It was hectic at times and often, very often, funny, such as the time in the Annapolis Valley when cameraman Jody Jessome and I were doing a story about a lady who lived close to a flour mill. She had been complaining that dust and seeds were blowing across the street onto her property, causing her health problems. We had completed the interview and were driving the lady along the main street of Kentville when a truck came out of a side street, through a stop sign and struck our news cruiser. I was in the back seat writing the script for my stand-up, Jody was driving and the elderly lady sat in the passenger seat.

We were shaken up. The lady had bumped her head on the windshield but even if we were all close to dying, I doubt the humour of the situation could have escaped us.

Two men jumped out of the truck. They were brothers just down from the mountain. They looked at our cruiser, which was well-identified with the big ATV logo, and then they looked at me.

"Bruce Graham," one brother whined to the other brother who had been driving. "You hit Bruce Graham." Then, to show his unhappiness with his brother's driving, he started beating on the front of their truck. He then informed us that his brother shouldn't be driving, that he couldn't drive worth shit. He said they'd just had an accident two weeks ago and he would surely lose his license this time.

"Bruce Graham, I can't believe you hit Bruce Graham."

Meanwhile, the driver confirmed everything his brother said. There was never a denial, even over the fact he couldn't drive worth shit. After which the brother who was the passenger reiterated that he couldn't believe they had been dumb enough to have hit Bruce Graham, as if I had half a dozen judges in my back pocket and one phone call would throw the pair of them into the slammer.

Ken Clark

While these humorous, high adventures were going on in my life, a quiet man by the name of Ken Clark was laying out a plan he had to the Irving brothers in Saint John. Ken Clark was manager of the Irving television station in Saint John and a former ATV salesman. He was an extremely diligent man and a hard worker. He had read CHUM's successful application regarding ASN. Clark saw a small but important distinction between a satellite service and a regular off-air television operation. Eventually, he would take that distinction to the CRTC as part of an application for a regular off-air television station in Dartmouth. He failed in his first attempt. Never discouraged, Ken redrew and refined the application. He resubmitted it to the CRTC and this time was successful. Maritime Independent Television, MITV, was born.

The Decision

When Ken Clark offered me the news director's job at a brand new station, the temptation was almost irresistible. After almost a decade at ATV I was ready for a new challenge. ATV had a strong hold on the ratings. We were established and I suppose I could have spent the next twenty years there. But I'm the type of restless spirit that needs new mountains to climb. The difficult aspect was leaving so many friends and colleagues. I had formed many alliances at ATV. Most have stood the test of time. Perhaps because I started in television operations or just as my natural inclination, most of my closest friends were camera and technical people. A bond of brothers had grown together over the years. We'd camp together, hold skeet shoots and we had many great times together.

When it was announced I had tendered my resignation, Heather Proudfoot, one of the most beautiful people I have ever known, cried in the newsroom and I felt awful, as if I was deserting the team. As it turned out, a lot of that team came with me.

10

Dartmouth, 1988

Getting MITV off the Ground

Television is a two-faced beast at the best of times. Don't let anyone tell you differently. While stations proclaim they are open to listeners' concerns, they are not really open at all. It's true, there are established channels for viewers' complaints, but they are mostly a sham. Oh, they'll listen to your complaint all right, as long as it doesn't interfere with making money.

Once, at ATV, I was working on a story about people and the mass media. I went upstairs to the executive offices and asked if they kept a file on viewers' comments. I was handed a very thick manila file, crammed with hundreds, if not thousands, of letters. I took the file back to my desk and started reading. Almost without exception every letter was a complaint and the complaints were on the same subject – intimate feminine products.

If you extrapolate those complaints, it would demonstrate that Canadians in the 1980s didn't want to see Kotex commercials in their living rooms. The letters seemed to be from a cross-section of society: men and women, well-spoken and plain-spoken. It didn't matter how much they complained or how many letters they wrote, their complaints went nowhere except into that file. I suggest to you that with the exception of cable television's billing fiasco, there has never been a single issue in Canadian broadcasting that prompted so many complaints. But it didn't matter what the viewers liked or didn't like. Money is money. That's the message you don't hear in the media.

One of my objectives at MITV was to try to give the viewer more of a voice in the message. To a certain extent, I'd had some success in doing that in Winnipeg by spending a lot of time on the streets of the city talking to people. At MITV I wanted to take the concept to a higher level, to establish street corner journalism. In other words, have the opinions come from ordinary people, not the conglomerate of spin from government, public relations and corporate Canada, who were controlling more and more of what got on the air.

The first thing was to find the niche we needed in news. We were competing against two highly successful stations. Although CBC had never matched ATV, it still ran a respectable news operation and had a fair share of the market. ATV was Maritimes, CBC was Nova Scotia, so the only avenue I saw for a new fledgling station was local, local, local. That meant metro Halifax-Dartmouth.

It turned out to be a good choice and the only choice we had anyway. It became evident very quickly that MITV didn't have enough power to reach the suburbs, let alone the rest of Nova Scotia. We had a sister station in Saint John that had a better reach in New Brunswick, but in Nova Scotia the coverage of our transmitter was grim. So we became the Halifax-Dartmouth metro station. We also offset our major news packages to 7 p.m. and 11 p.m.

Hiring

We were flooded with applications. People who had never been in a television station applied for a job, old men, young women, old women and young men. We received over seven hundred applications for the eighty-five jobs available. It turned out I wasn't the only person who felt the need for a new challenge. Many of the applications came from ATV. In my mind, that goes to show you that working in a station that is a long-time market leader can have certain drawbacks.

Some people find it stifling in an environment where they've reached the apex of the market. Some of the staff found Dick Prat's management style dictatorial, although personally I didn't. Dick and I certainly had our disagreements, but I respected him and with Dick you always knew where you stood. Some bosses are far less honest and certainly less forthright.

There's another theory at play as well. Staying on top isn't as creative an experience as getting to the top. I suspect that's why some of the leading ATV on-air people took a chance and crossed the harbour to Dartmouth, to an old mattress factory that was soon to become MITV.

I hired Laura Lee Langley to co-anchor the major newscast with me. Donnie Verge and Chuck Stewart came aboard as did news cameramen Wayne Clark, Jamie Munro and Ian Chisholm. Donnie Verge was made operations manager and he brought more people from ATV. Chuck was production boss and he did the same. When we went on the air on Labour Day, 1988, there were twenty-one news staffers in my department; seven were from ATV.

It was well publicized that we were going on air Labour Day but we very nearly didn't make it. Two weeks before the launch date it appeared to be an impossible goal. Part of our transmitter was sitting on a tarmac somewhere in France and another piece was in California. Our master control wasn't wired, editing suites weren't completed. Technical people were working around the clock. People had to learn their jobs and become acquainted with new equipment. The control room wasn't ready and wires spewed everywhere. Strangers, apparently important visitors, were walking through the mounds of wire and watching the bedlam and probably thinking, "What a madhouse!"

There was no question the final days looked like chaos. The Irvings sent in one of their troubleshooters – a type of Mr. Fix-it with a reputation for getting things done. That man could certainly work the phones, calling contacts all over the continent, getting a rare piece of equipment or a specialized cable or a gadget here and a gadget there. It was like putting a giant jigsaw puzzle together. The last piece was ready about 6:30 Labour Day morning. With staff, family and press, Ken Clark pushed the button promptly at 7 a.m. and Maritime Independent Television was on the air. Eastern

Canada had a new television station. Twelve hours later, our first major newscast would be broadcast.

I remembered when the CanWest station in Winnipeg signed on the air for the first time. On their first newscast, the video was upside down. Someone had loaded the film incorrectly in the projector. What I didn't want was a similar glaring error. There was so much riding on us getting off to a smooth start with new equipment and new people and there was too much that could go wrong. I decided to do something seldom done in local television news.

My plan was that we should tape our first newscast a half hour early and if we had problems, then we could go live at seven. On the other hand, if the tape went flawlessly and everything worked we'd simply play the tape. The newscast went well, the broadcast was flawless and we ran it.

The next day the newspapers got hold of the fact we'd taped our newscast and made some snide comments. Apparently, they didn't realize that for years the CBC National news was taped every night, but no matter, the next night we were live and looking like we knew what we were doing.

The fact is, if we had started out as the laughingstock of the industry it would have been even more difficult for a news staff, who we were asking to pull off an almost incredible accomplishment – to attract and keep an audience in the wake of keen competition. Remember we started out with absolutely no audience and had to build from zero. We knew it would take time and commitment. But broadcasting our news at seven instead of six gave us better ratings than we expected. Considering our transmitter couldn't reach all of outlying Sackville, our ratings at seven were fairly respectable for a new station. We were doing stories the other stations were ignoring and that was helping too. We weren't the biggest and maybe we weren't the best, but we were carving out a niche for ourselves in the market.

Changes and More Changes

Then a whole series of events happened that changed MITV forever. Fifteen months later, the Irvings decided to sell. They looked at the bottom line of the fledging operation and saw there was more profit in selling than in operating the Saint John and Dartmouth stations over the next number of years. The theory is, in the world of television you have to be a big player. Stand-alone stations, unless they are part of a major chain or have an alliance with big media corporations, have trouble surviving because of programming costs. The Irvings must have known this fact when they initially applied for the television license. Maybe the profit picture just wasn't there or maybe CanWest made them an offer they couldn't refuse. Regardless, to our surprise they announced they were selling MITV to CanWest Global. I was immediately alarmed. I had seen Global television in its infancy in Winnipeg, and it was evident with a cursory glance that it wasn't spending much money on its local programming – particularly its news.

Global's Birth Pangs

Global Television was the near bankrupt Toronto enterprise of founders Al Bruner and Peter Hill. They signed on the air in January of 1974. By the following March they were in receivership, losing an estimated $50,000 a day. Global was to be the flagship for independent television stations, an alliance that could buy and share programming. Izzy Asper, Paul Morton, Seymour Epstein and Allan Slaight came to the rescue. They saved the station but not their partnership. Slaight was out and so eventually was Morton. I'm not interested in rehashing the corporate history of CanWest. The short story is Izzy Asper won the grand prize and gained control of Global. He fought another protracted lawsuit for control of Vancouver television station CKVU. He won that one too.

There was no question Asper was aggressive and fearless. As I say, I had watched him from my days in Winnipeg. I had interviewed him when he was the Manitoba Liberal leader and I was keenly interested in the development of his first television station CKND. I wasn't an expert on Izzy Asper, but I had some idea of how he worked and his corporate mentality. It caused me grave concern for the future of MITV.

Izzy Asper

While many flowery words have been written about Izzy Asper, some of them paid for by Asper himself, from my perspective I didn't see an accomplished tycoon but a disseminator and destroyer of local news programming.

Today in the lobby of Global stations there is plaque on the wall listing the accomplishments of the company founder. This mini-shrine lists Asper's accomplishments. It reads: Husband, Father, Grandfather, Brother, Friend, Musician, Visionary, Entrepreneur, Broadcaster, Politician, Advocate, Philanthropist, Patriot, Champion, Founder, Intellectual, Mogul, Journalist, Lawyer, Challenger – I.H. Asper 1932-2003

Aside from the egregious egotism, there is no doubt Izzy Asper had the ability to accumulate money. He was a driven corporate visionary, but in the world of Canadian television is it really that much of an accomplishment to fill your broadcast day with cheap U.S. programming? There is no question Asper had chutzpah, but his corporate slash and burn methods left many local newsrooms in shambles. Izzy Asper may be many things, but a cultural icon who promoted Canadian news or Canadian programming, he was definitely not.

When it was learned MITV would fall into the hands of Global, my only hope was that maybe in the intervening years since Winnipeg, the corporate philosophy of Global had changed. Hindsight shows my initial suspicions were correct. In 2007, Global announced yet another major cut at MITV, laying off a goodly percent of the staff. This was just one of several layoffs putting people with young families out of work by a company trying to squeeze a few more dollars on its multi-million-dollar profit margin. The weakened MITV newsroom stopped documentary work and investigative reporting.

If you read the original promise of performance of MITV submitted by Ken Clark in the license application to the CRTC, you would see viewers were promised a fine arts program, a business show, expanded news and public affairs plus other local programming. Ken Clark was an extremely hard worker with strong ethics. Had he not left MITV to be general manager of CKY Winnipeg (my former station), everything he promised would have been done. Managers change and so do owners and as so often happens in broadcasting, promises made by solemn-faced men in dark suits before the CRTC can fly away faster than down on a thistle, demonstrating once again a promise of performance isn't worth the paper it's written on.

I give Global some credit. It has added a national newscast and it's pretty good and some nights it's much better than any similar broadcast, but it hardly makes up for the lack of local coverage and decimated newsrooms from Vancouver to Dartmouth.

The blame for such abysmal shirking of corporate responsibility and the lack of local news lies with the Canadian Radio and Television and Telecommunication Commission, the body that oversees broadcasting. The CRTC has believed the bleating of crybaby corporations – broadcasters like CanWest Global that rake in millions – that they simply can't afford to do more Canadian programming. To make matters worse, on at least one occasion when CanWest got a decision it didn't like from the CRTC, it appealed directly to the federal cabinet and the politicians overruled their own agency. God, don't you love Canada?

CanWest has taken more from broadcasting and given less to Canadian viewers than any other corporation, but it certainly isn't alone in the shameful lack of Canadian content on Canadian airwaves.

The Great Wait

After the announcement of the sale to CanWest there were many months of waiting for the finalization of the purchase by the new owners. It was an unsettling time for the MITV staff. We were in a period of incredible transition without knowing what our future held. The old owners were going and the new owners had not yet officially taken control. The company drifted without a great deal of direction. Bickering broke out among staff members – former friends who had crossed the harbour from ATV hardly spoke to each other. Tension was high and the initial euphoria was rapidly disappearing.

Global brought in Larry Nichols from Toronto to run the ship and in many ways he did significant work. But he spent most of his time in Saint John when a strong hand was required at the helm in Dartmouth. Then Nichols did something that tore the bottom out of the major news package at 7:00 p.m. He moved it to 6:00, directly against ATV and CBC. Overnight, the bottom fell out of our news ratings and our morale plummeted even more. It was a major blow at a time of uncertainty and it did nothing to improve working conditions.

I tried to weather through the disappointment around me. I said nothing of my earlier observation of Asper's Winnipeg operation. People knew. We had started on such a high note and it seemed we were now in free fall. But I had a leadership role to fulfill and a newsroom to run. We tinkered with the new program in a mad effort to attract some viewers. The decision was to split the hour into two parts and two distinct programs.

The first half hour would be all local. Doug Vasin joined Laura Lee Langley on the anchor desk and I took over the second half hour, which we totally devoted to national and world news plus my evening commentary. Thus the Graham Report was born. Besides running the newsroom and occasionally going into the field, I continued to anchor a half-hour daily news broadcast and write a nightly commentary. Shifting to the world scene there was plenty to cover.

Despite poor ratings, we sought out exclusive stories. We did a number of documentaries and did them well, which gained us recognition for doing first-class work.

John's Story was about a week in the life of an alcoholic, a man on the streets with no real home and no money except what he could beg by panhandling. It was a powerful, gritty program. Some found it difficult to watch and not every viewer approved of our efforts. We were criticized by some viewers for exploiting the poor man.

Wade Keller was the young photo journalist who walked the streets and back alleys with John. His camera told the story. There weren't any other editorial comments by us. It was just John, his drinking buddies and his point of view. I'm happy to report that the last time I saw John he was on the road to recovery. He'd stopped drinking and was getting his life back in order. He'd been down into the depths of hell and come back. Plenty of the people who saw his story were willing to help him instead of condemning us.

A documentary that won us a national award was *Proud People of Our Coast*. The hour-long documentary was the story of the people in Canso and Shelburne in Nova Scotia and Trepassey in Newfoundland. These three fishing communities faced extremely hard times. Kelly Ryan wrote and produced the program, Wayne Clark shot it and I was host. We travelled to the communities, interviewed fishermen and fish plant workers. The inshore fishery was dying and there was plenty of finger-pointing and blistering attacks against federal fisheries policies, foreign trawlers and big offshore draggers tearing up the ocean floor. In Newfoundland, the mayor of Trepassey threatened to chain herself to the wharf as a show of protest.

The program was full of tears and strained voices but it touched something far deeper. It revealed the agony that a way of life was ending, that the oceans could not be relied upon to be plundered indefinitely. There wasn't as much known about climate change then as there is today but there was already the awareness that something in the sea was wrong, whether it was foreign fishing, mismanagement or scraping and raping the ocean bottom. You could see it in the eyes of mothers who worried about their children's future and their husbands' well-being. Seven generations of fishermen had known plenty of hardship, but this was different.

They all knew something out there in that great expanse of ocean was gravely wrong. They carried it with them in their expressions. You could hear it in their voices.

We were the passive onlookers. The people were the story and their expressions and words won Best News Documentary at the Atlantic Film Festival.

We covered murder stories, of course, some of them crazy killings by whacked-out people on cocaine or some other hallucinogen. Who shoots a man on Gottingen Street then hails a cab for a two-block ride, jumps in the back seat and says loud enough for the driver to hear, "They can't cheat Smokey Smith and get away with it."? Needless to say, Smokey wasn't at large for long.

It's the families of both the victim and the perpetrator who often wear most of the misery of the crime, hanging their heads in court with the victim on one side, accused on the other. Sometimes the two sides clash in the hallway, with more fisticuffs, name-calling, tears and misery. How many times in forty years have I heard the mother of a murderer say the same words while trying to grasp at a reason when there is no reason and when there is simply nothing else to say? No matter what her son has done, what heinous crimes he's committed, a weeping mother utters the mantra of all mothers, "He's a good boy."

Your mother always loves you when no one else does.

Our work was not all negatives. There were inspiring stories too. Stories that earned our respect because they made us pay attention to them. They gave us a reason to lift our heads from the daily grind to see the goodness of people. Reporting on the noble human spirit made our jobs more worthwhile, although I'm not in favour of running around looking for stories that are necessarily good news. The best stories happen because a man, woman or child has risen above and beyond the norm. Here's an example.

Commentary: Life

Every once in a while a news story touches those of us who toil in this business. We are basically immune to sensitivity. It's not that we're uncaring as much as that we could never do our jobs if we got personally attached to each and every human crisis that swirls around us, hour after hour. But sometimes even the toughest hide gets pricked by a particular set of circumstances, such as the one that touched me.

A Nova Scotia father plunges into the water to save his own child and the child of his fiancée. The two boys, twelve and thirteen, were swimming near the mouth of the Lawrencetown River near Dartmouth and riptides are strong. The undertow started to take the boys out to sea and Laurie Boucher and his fiancée rescued them, but Boucher couldn't get back himself. That was Saturday. He hasn't been seen since.

Many people might think twice about jumping into the water to save a stranger, but to save their own child, the most modest in strength can muster mighty courage.

That's not to take away from Mr. Boucher and his heroic act. It's just to reiterate the bond between child and parent, often strained and fragmented, still remains the strongest bond of all.

I have friends who haven't spoken to their adult daughter in years. A family falling out, but they still love her, still know deep within themselves they would risk all to save her. Children give us many things, from great joy to great frustration. They also make us uneasy, exposed, knowing we would jump or dash or rush to save them, risking ourselves totally. Maybe it's difficult for any parent not to silently shiver when hearing of the story of Laurie Boucher. Maybe we are him and he is us, connected by that common worldwide brotherhood and sisterhood, known as – parents.

* * *

Some commentaries unexpectedly garnered an unusual amount of feedback. Maybe it was because the topic dealt with words and animals, maybe the fun I was having with the subject was contagious. The public's response can be fickle and unpredictable. Certain things, certain issues just touch people. The reaction prompted me to write a follow-up.

Commentary: Words and Animals

A couple of months ago, I wrote a commentary on the names of groupings of animals such as a murder of crows, a pod of whales and a parliament of owls. The subject drew response from viewers in phone calls and letters and even moved a retired school-teacher from New Brunswick to send me this fascinating book called *An Exaltation of Larks*. It puts groupings on a whole new level and moves beyond the animal kingdom with over 10,000 terms from plumbers to priests and back again. Here are a few examples.

A charge of shoppers, a generation of sperm banks, a quick chance of New Year's resolutions. In the professions we have a chisel of repairmen, an OHM of electricians, a flush of plumbers.

There's more, many more. A snooze of night watchmen is one of my favourites. How about a ring of jewelers, an aroma of bakers? Also, an ambush of used car dealers.

Some of these groups sound so appropriate, don't they? Some are just fun. An ingratitude of children. A mutter of mothers-in-law, an eyesore of graffiti, a rot of garbage or an indifference of waiters and a spill of bus boys.

The book is called *An Exaltation of Larks* by James Lipton. The publisher is Viking Press. So, from an Audi-cue of anchors and a wind of weather guys, we now say good night to you, an eyeball of viewers.

11

Controversies, 1989–1992

I became embroiled in two public controversies during my first years at MITV. In many respects they were related to each other. The first had to do with the touchy subject of news embargoes.

A news embargo is imposed by someone who wants the media to know something but wants to control when the public knows it. The initial use of embargoes was for provincial and federal budgets and in that sense they hold some value, since a budget is a multi-paged document that needs some time for study and clarification. I've participated in both provincial and federal budgets and it's easy to understand the merit of such embargoes.

What the Nova Scotia government was doing in the 1980s was something entirely different. Politicians were using embargoes as a way of reviewing proposed legislation. In more than one case, reporters attending an embargoed news briefing pointed out serious flaws and the bills were withdrawn. The reporters went away and the matter was dropped. The reporters were conspiratorial in covering up the government's blunder. Because they had agreed to the embargo, they couldn't report anything of the event. That situation was all right with a lot of people at Province House, but the relationship between the press and the politicians was a whole lot more incestuous than I thought was healthy.

Hugo Black, American Supreme Court Justice, once said, "Only a free and unrestrained press can effectively expose deception in government." But how is deception exposed if the press is so intimate with government it freely vets proposed legislation and keeps quiet about it?

Peter Jennings once wrote, "If what we do as journalists is to act as witnesses, then I want to be in the front seat." But at Province House, the front seats were taken up by journalists who were silently compliant and complicit. To make matter worse, such compliance was spreading. In the 1980s the use of embargoed material grew year by year. We'd receive press releases on our fax machine or hand-delivered by public relations companies with bold letters written across the top: "EMBARGOED UNTIL 6 P.M. JANUARY 24." Says who? That's what I wanted to know. Who has the right to give me a piece of information and order me to hold it for their convenience? Municipal governments and federal departments jumped into the practice of issuing embargoed material. Please report this when we say it is all right to report it.

I had never been a fan of embargoes in the news business and had deliberately broken some in Winnipeg. Ten years later, the practice was out of control. It was time to take a stand. I made the editorial decision that I knew would have some unwelcome consequences. We would respect budget lock-ups but would not honour other news embargoes. Frankly, it was more a public relations risk than a journalistic one. Most of the material you got in embargoes was far from earth-shaking. If the government had really important news for the public, particularly if it made the government look good, we'd get it anyway. It's called reporting.

It wasn't surprising that most of the flak over our decision came from other reporters, not the public. The regulars at Province House belong to a little club called the Nova Scotia Press Gallery. They're the ones very chummy with elected representatives. The press gallery – that clubby little clique of reporters – took me to task for my stand as did some of the PR firms, but it didn't hurt our news broadcasts one iota. It also saved some ink in our fax machine. But the press gallery was seething. After some blustering they threatened to evict MITV from the gallery, although we were a paid-up member.

As I recall, they finally did kick us out but it didn't matter because by that time there was another challenge, albeit a part of the same problem of openness and accountability. While the press gallery was giving us the boot, Premier John Buchanan was making animal noises in the legislature. He was either clucking like a chicken or squealing like a pig. Spectators in the gallery were disgusted by such shenanigans

This was just another sign that something was very wrong with Nova Scotia's seat of government. The legislature was closed to cameras with press gallery reporters acting as unofficial public relations flacks for MLAs. It was way past time to open up the proceedings of the legislature and let all Nova Scotians have a front-row seat.

I went to Larry Nichols, the new general manager who replaced Ken Clark. I had an idea that would require his support and the company's money. I suspected rough waters ahead. To launch my plan would mean a hard legal fight that would pit MITV against the Speaker of the Legislature, the Premier and the entire Buchanan government, who were used to getting their own way and making their own rules. They were the supreme council, the governing body who looked after their friends, had given themselves gold-plated pensions and plenty of vacation time. They had refused previous requests to have the legislature's proceedings televised. I had no doubt the government of Nova Scotia would use taxpayers' dollars to fight us tooth and nail.

We hired the services of a media lawyer and in July of 1989 MITV launched a legal action in the trial division of the Supreme Court of Nova Scotia against the Buchanan government, demanding the right to place television cameras in the Nova Scotia Legislature.

The reaction was predictable and pathetically funny. Initially, the biggest complaint concerning our desire to open up the legislature was the concern of politicians that the television camera would expose dozing, nose-picking MLAs.

Ah, er, exposure. Isn't that exactly the point? Television would increase decorum, not eradicate it. It was almost nonexistent anyway. By the time we went to court in November of '89, the CBC had joined our cause. We were co-plaintiffs against the government.

And so began a two-year journey through the courts. The government fought vigorously. After all, they had to protect those nose-pickers, pig-squealers and nappers from being noticed. What better way to spend taxpayers' money? Mr. Justice Hilroy

Nathanson heard the case in the trial division. In May of 1990 he ruled in our favour, stating that indeed under the law we did have a right to access to the legislature from the gallery with our own portable camera.

That should have been the end of it. We won and were willing to sit down with the Speaker and discuss an unobtrusive approach to television in the legislature. We even offered to provide a raw pool feed for our competitors. By then, those dozing in the legislature were fully awake. Accustomed to a compliant press gallery they could control, they didn't want to give the media so much power. But how could they control the pictures when they didn't control the camera or the camera operator? Suddenly, from a government that wasn't interested in television, there was serious discussion of the government spending hundreds of thousands of dollars on its own TV system. Remember, this was taxpayers' money and they were prepared to spend it on a system we were prepared to supply for free, but with one very important distinction – controlling the point of view.

While they were pondering the possibilities, they had to do something with the decision of Mr. Justice Nathanson. They decided to appeal the decision, meaning another round of legal proceedings in the court of appeal.

Arthur Donahoe was the Speaker of the Legislature and it fell on him to represent the Buchanan government. He took the oath and testified. He begged for time to consult with all members of the legislature and the rest of the press gallery, who would have to be considered. He said public money would have to be spent even though we had offered to provide a pool feed to all broadcasters.

The appeal by the government was dismissed with Mr. Justice Freeman writing, "So long as the camera is neither too pervasive nor too obtrusive, there can be no good reason for excluding it." Whether it was pervasive or obtrusive was to be decided by the House of Assembly or the Speaker on its behalf.

So, despite all the legislative foot-dragging, we had won the right in two courts of law to take our camera into the legislature, set up in the gallery overlooking the proceedings and tape those proceedings. We would do so quietly, with decorum and dignity and make the business of the House open to the public. We would use wide shots and close ups and we were again prepared to sit down with the Speaker and work out some rules.

This was all a nightmare for the MLAs. They would have to put away the crossword puzzles and actually pay attention. It would be harder to play hooky or snooze at their desks.

Meanwhile, by this time television cameras had moved into the House of Commons. The system was restrictive, allowing only shots of the individual Member of Parliament speaking and absolutely no reaction shots. Viewers had little idea how empty the chamber actually was most of the time. It's better today, although the government still controls the shots as if the Commons were a private country club and not the peoples' business. It's hardly the free-flowing system I would endorse where the viewer can scan the Commons at any time to see what their own MP is doing.

Here's an early commentary I wrote on television and the House of Commons.

Commentary: Speaking in the Void

I don't know if you ever watch the parliamentary channel that brings Canadians the comings and goings of the House of Commons. Since most of the seats seem empty most of the time, there seems to be more going than coming.

Our Maritime Members of Parliament can be seen from time to time giving a speech and waving some papers in the air, putting on their best performances for the television cameras. Since there is usually no one sitting around them, the TV camera is all they can play to.

It's bad enough that the speeches are long, but I keep wanting to know who's sitting in the Commons. It's time they took the restrictions off parliamentary TV. After all, are we not mature enough to see our Commons as it is? If the seats are empty, they're empty. How can we trust an institution that refuses to show Canadians how many Members are sitting in the House? Let's take the restrictions off parliamentary television, let's have wide shots and long shots and overhead shots. Let's see who's there, and let's see if my MP's speech is having any impact on anybody else.

There may be an excuse for the parliamentary channel being

boring. There is no excuse for it being dishonest and for refusing to show Canadians the real picture, which is the entire picture.

* * *

That was my feeling then and as it remains today. How can we trust an institution that refuses to show us the real picture? I wrote to Speaker Donahoe that we were prepared to cooperate with the legislature and to follow the rules set down in the decision by Mr. Justice Nathanson. We would guarantee our camera would be unobtrusive and not create any undue interruptions to the proceedings of the House. The government was having none of it. By then, after losing two court decisions, they understood cameras were coming but, by God, if they couldn't fend them off they would totally control them.

They appealed the court's decision to the Supreme Court of Canada. By then, politicians from other provinces were jumping on the bandwagon to oppose us. Seven provincial legislatures had joined the fray, supporting their counterparts in Nova Scotia. The Speaker from Saskatchewan, Arnold Tusa, declared the case involved crucial issues such as the authority of the Speaker to maintain order and decorum. Newfoundland Speaker Thomas Lush voiced similar support, arguing the House had exclusive jurisdiction in matters related to internal proceedings. Ontario Speaker David Warner stated if the Nova Scotia decision was enforced it would impair his ability to control the internal workings of the Ontario legislature.

They were all fallacious arguments. Actually, a free and open airing of proceedings under public scrutiny would enhance the workings of the House, not hinder them. The Canadian Association of Journalists requested intervenor status and so did the Speaker of the Commons John Fraser. If the Supreme Court ruled against them, other television stations in other provinces could follow our lead.

The provinces won in the Supreme Court of Canada but by then in Nova Scotia it hardly mattered. The Buchanan government had rushed to establish its own very safe procedure for television in the legislative assembly. The tight shot shows the MLA addressing the legislature but whether the room is full or empty is impossible to determine. Since that time they have relented a bit but still the other side can whistle and squeal across the aisle without fear of having such antics shown on television. They made sure of that.

The end result of our litigation allowed cameras in the legislature. In that we were successful, even though it was not the system I envisioned. There are no camera swings around the legislature, no cutaways. It was, and still is, rigidity television.

It is worth noting that a buddy-buddy press does not uncover many stories that really matter. Oh, they report on the normal activities but they do not delve into the deep pool of self-serving initiatives, lethargy and corruption that inevitably hangs around the neck of old administrations.

Governments are not similar to fine wine; they do not improve with age. Governments are more like the human body with an accelerated aging process. After one term they age quickly, become frail and forgetful. By their third term they are lame and often fart publicly. In terms of a political life the Buchanan government was old and suffering. It had invested in money-losing companies, put taxpayers' dollars into high-tech toilet seats and approved a bridge in Cape Breton that went nowhere. A more rigorous press might have sooner exposed such deficiencies. My experience with television cameras in the legislature demonstrates that politicians will do anything to keep the public at arm's length. They still do.

And finally, I know many people in journalism will take issue with my assessment. I only remind them of the words of George Orwell: "Freedom is the right to tell people what they do not want to hear."

12

Changing of the Guard, 1992

In 1992, Larry Nichols called me into his office. I was losing my position as Director of News and Public Affairs. He felt it was time for a change in news management and frankly, I agreed with him. I was totally frustrated we couldn't reach more viewers. No matter how diligent you are in television, if people can't reach your station you're working in a vacuum. After four years of incredible challenges, with a disillusioned staff and lack of a sense of direction partly due to a change in ownership, I'd had enough. I would remain as commentator and anchor of the major newscast and would take the position of executive producer with the mission of building new public affairs programming for the company. There was a catch to the new position that I only understood a week later. Not only did I have to develop new programming, but I also had to find sponsors for it.

Anchorman, commentator and now suddenly a salesman.

John O'Brien took over the news director's position and in less than two years he was fired. It was the only time in almost forty years in broadcasting I've seen an employee treated in such a fashion. John came to work one morning to find his office key would not fit in his door. During the night, management had the locks to his office changed. There he stood in his trench coat expecting to put in another day at work but he was as locked out of a job as he was locked out of his office. It was a petty, stupid thing to do and my respect for the company decreased another notch.

Soon there was another unfathomable act from management. Laura Lee Langley was taken off the 6 p.m. news and put on the late night news. She was replaced by Judy Pal. Judy was a competent broadcaster, but it was a move no one could understand and it only added to the chaos spinning around the newsroom. I kept my head down and worked on my commentaries. It was like being in some low-grade horror film with no plot, no theme and frankly, was just plain crazy.

Fortunately, there was plenty of news to take my mind off my work environment. John Savage was premier and his government was almost as chaotic as our newsroom. I had known Savage for years and used to call him Mr. Premier when he was a practicing physician in Dartmouth. I did so because I knew, as many others did, that he had an interest in politics and had run unsuccessfully for the Liberal party. When I heard he was running for the leadership of the Nova Scotia Liberal party I had my doubts about his success. I thought he could win the leadership all right, but I doubted his style would go over with rural Liberals. On that account I was absolutely right. John Savage had very high ideals, but high ideals don't save you from being done in by your own party.

Savage had a penchant for getting into trouble politically. One of his concepts was public-private partnerships. This was a way for the construction of public buildings by private enterprise. The plan might have worked if schools hadn't been included. The public seemed to hate the idea of their kids' schools turned into a private business, where they had to pay a private company to have students use the gym at night. While Rodney MacDonald revived the idea in 2008, in the '90s when Savage tried the idea it was met with wave after wave of public hostility.

Then there was the Halifax casino. A similar facility was built in Cape Breton but it didn't attract the controversy of the Halifax operation. The casino idea drew criticism from the minute it was announced, despite the government's flaunting the big cheque it was getting from American operators. Some hated the idea and organized rallies and public meetings. Social activists said the gambling would only increase problems in our society and lead to addictions, family breakup and suicide, all of which has pretty well come true.

Savage and his government would not back down. He lost brownie points and his popularity diminished, but the deck had been cut and the casinos would be built.

And built they were, but not without more controversy. Construction got way behind schedule. The operators, ITT Sheraton, should have been paying millions in penalties for not meeting the construction schedule, but the Premier's Office intervened. Now there was controversy inside a controversy. Those against said they told you so; those in favour called it a glitch. I called it a political boondoggle.

Commentary: Gaming

In Nova Scotia we are having a sort of casino-gate controversy here, where the province and Premier's Office intervened, over the head of its Gaming Corporation, and let ITT Sheraton off the hook for some $20 million in penalties it should have paid for being late in starting its big casino on the Halifax waterfront. Ahh! Life is a gamble.

Yesterday the gaming people took a gamble and shot back. They staged a two-and-a-half-hour news conference where they tried to stretch the credulity of every man, woman and child in the province. Either the people at the Nova Scotia Gaming Corporation are incredibly naïve, or they think the rest of us are incredibly gullible.

First, there is the question of timing. Ralph Fiske, the former head of the Gaming Corporation, the man who brought all this to the public, was back today before the legislative committee to answer more questions. So, just the day before he testifies, the Gaming Corporation holds its own news conference and tells us the timing is coincidental. Making statements in public is a gamble.

Then they claim the Gaming Corporation is a hard bargainer, that it was not outmatched and outmaneuvered by the Sheraton. Defending yourself is a gamble.

What people bring minutes of their meetings to a news conference and then expect reporters to sign promises they won't make those minutes public? Showing your naivety is definitely a gamble. Then there is the question of semantics. The Gaming Corporation says it's autonomous from government, but not independent of government. Huh? Autonomous means functioning independently. So they're saying we are independent but we're not. We are and we aren't: we're both a duck and a chicken.

The Gaming Corporation didn't refute the charges of Ralph Fiske yesterday. What it did accomplish was to paint itself as naïve about the rest of us and confused about itself. Mr. Fiske didn't have to say anything to increase his credibility.

You can't be both a chicken and a duck.

* * *

I might have given Savage a little heat but I genuinely liked the man. He was a humanitarian and an internationalist. His humanitarian efforts in Cuba drew cold silences from the United States. But I liked that about him. However, that penchant for trouble seemed to follow him like a dark cloud. Once in 1996 when I was in a poetic mood, I wrote an ode to John Savage.

Commentary: Ode to Savage

Tonight, an ode to John Savage, Premier, traveller, terminator and trade promoter. It goes like this:

Our Premier he travels – trade is his game,
But wherever he goes the world goes insane.
He went to Cuba as the planes were shot down,
Destabilizing the dollar and threatening the pound.
The trade mission's a bust – with new sanctions galore,
The U.S. is angry and promising more.
Not the least dejected with that heated dispute,
The Premier was soon off on another trade toot.
This time it's China, with its wall and its junks,
Its aging old leaders and its New Age young punks.
China's people may trade but they surely can't vote
And hopes of democracy seem fairly remote.
But as the Premier digests his first won ton
All hell breaks out in nearby Taiwan.

Warships and chatter and tensions and fear,
The Premier's trade group slips down to low gear.
Two trips and two hot spots – and Savage is there.
His trips have more intrigue than a current affair.
Nice as it is to get away for the snow
Peacemakers everywhere say – Premier, don't go.
They may love you or hate you on your own turf
But your travels are threatening peace on this earth.
Please, Mr. Savage, for world peace we bemoan,
Forget all this travel and simply stay home.

* * *

John Savage's biggest political mistake originated from his soft heart. He had no time for politics as usual but plenty of time for the downtrodden. Except this mistake cost the people of Nova Scotia dearly. The Savage government was faced with its biggest challenge when a group of men went public, claiming that as young inhabitants of provincial institutions they were verbally, physically and sexually abused while incarcerated. The men wanted compensation from the Nova Scotia government for the mistreatment.

Before the government could respond, more and more alleged victims joined the chorus, until suddenly it seemed every child ever institutionalized was in some way abused. Their numbers grew day by day and so did their clamour. They had no proof but they had plenty of voices. They held news conferences and gave interviews. Some of them seemed legitimate and some seemed less so, but how could you separate the truth from the fiction? How do you prove or disprove something that happened ten or twenty years ago? The Savage government just wanted the issue to go away so it offered compensation. That offer opened the floodgates for more men to come forward. The cost was now in the millions and the government's action besmirched the reputation of innocent people who had worked at the institutions. If the people accused of mistreatment were truly innocent they could sue the government on their own behalf, which is exactly what they ultimately did.

After Savage was out of office, John Hamm's Conservative

government ordered an inquiry to see how such a blunder could have happened. I believe this was my last commentary on the subject.

Commentary: Review

The latest chapter in the ongoing Nova Scotia abuse case happened this week when the Hamm government announced a $1 million review into why the Liberals threw more millions at people who claimed they were abused at provincial institutions with no proof, no collaboration, no investigation. It was a grand money giveaway that branded innocent employees of these institutions as sexual deviants and abusive monsters.

You know the story. It's a mess and now we're spending a million dollars more to try to find out why people were so dumb, why people lied to get money, how innocent people got branded, why Nova Scotia always looks like the boondoggle province where we just came down from the mountain on the horse cart.

We don't need a million-dollar study for a Quebec judge to tell us we screwed up. The Hamm government could have demonstrated solid leadership but it's a mess so they did what Nova Scotia governments always do in such circumstances: call a review, a judicial inquiry, a royal commission.

We have volumes of moldy paper turning yellow in storage rooms from such studies. Has it made us a smarter province? I think not. We have had a police investigation and now another investigation. The Hamm government has simply passed the buck to a retired judge. The bottom line on any review can range anywhere from imprudent decision-making to rampant stupidity.

Spend the million on schools or health care rather than another review telling us how dumb we are. Most of us already know.

* * *

John Savage had to resign in March of 1997 after he served just four years. His party was in near revolt and the people of Nova Scotia disapproved of his programs. His Welsh accent didn't sit well in Antigonish and many found his manner arrogant. He was a doctor who cut health care. He thumbed his nose at party hacks who wanted to fire Tory road workers. Savage strongly declared that the era of patronage in Nova Scotia was over. He supported libraries and started the Dartmouth Book Awards, he tried to find ways to build more schools and he was dealing with a ballooning debt, much of it inherited from the Buchanan years. John Savage wasn't a man of the people but he was a man for the people. He was, I believe, a terrible politician, but a very good man.

The Media in the 1990s

On the world stage in the 1990s the media reports seemed as odd as the events whirling around it. The important was often trivialized and the trivial was often made earth-shaking. Hundreds of thousands of Rwandans were being butchered. Men, women and children were hacked to pieces in a genocide perpetrated by their own countrymen, but that never captured as much ink or air time as lesser stories.

The U.S. networks went crazy with Monica Lewinsky and the stain on her dress. Of course, Lewinsky was all about sex and the president's sex at that. Many Canadians were obsessed with the story too. It was the discussion around the office water cooler. After all, was it sex or wasn't it? Is oral sex, sex, or not sex? If not sex why is it called oral sex? Bill Clinton, who may be an expert on the subject, says no, oral is oral and sex is sex and never the thong shall meet. We all had our say. Here's mine in a commentary from August 1998.

Commentary: Stained Relations

"I did not have sexual relations with that woman, Miss Lewinsky," Bill Clinton declared on January 26th. The story gets more bizarre with each passing month. Last week, for example, a military band played in the Rose Garden, drowning out reporters' shouts to Clinton about Lewinsky's testimony before a grand jury. It had the surrealistic look of the last days of Richard Nixon.

There are plenty of similar Nixonian plots and subplots and many, far weirder. Such as: is oral sex outside sexual relations? So when the president of the United States says he did not have sexual relations with that woman, is he talking orally, or just talking nonsense? It's not only talking, it's how you talk.

Harry Thomason, a TV producer, moved into the White House and coached Bill Clinton on how to clench his jaw while delivering his strongest denial on Lewinsky.

And speaking of denials, where is Hillary through this long hot summer? At one time she was her husband's strongest defender, appearing on TV talk shows, claiming the scandal was all a plot by the American right wing. Hillary has all but vanished.

Later this month, Bill Clinton testifies via video to a grand jury. He is using video because he doesn't want to be seen as the first president walking into a courtroom – as opposed to the first president to be hounded and haunted by sex and a stain on a dress.

"I did not have sexual relations with that woman." Another catchword of Clinton's second term. The catchwords that may catch Clinton.

* * *

I wrote five commentaries a week that covered a range of subjects from Meech Lake to Mickey Mouse. I ranted on everything from politics to prisons to pensions. I supported the gays and that brought Christian condemnation. I condemned the powerful and that brought middle-class applause. If I made an error I admitted it. My goal was to get people thinking and sometimes I was successful. At times I strayed away from the usual newsy subjects to broach things such as suicide. I also dealt with the subject of death and society's peculiar reaction to it.

One example I used was the sudden death of Princess Diana, who died in a high-speed car crash in Paris. I had met her shortly after her marriage to the Prince of Wales. I thought she was very young and quite shy for such a heavy responsibility that already lay on her shoulders. She was popular with the British public but after her death she was elevated to an icon. The elevation was not exactly smooth.

Commentary: Death is so Final

Have you noticed a trend in our society? When you're first dead, they say the nicest things about you, then the tide turns and nice turns to mean.

Princess Diana has been riding a wave of public love and sympathy since her tragic death. But death leaves her unprotected. Libel laws protect the living but not the dead. For the famous, it means any drubbing is fair game. Your reputation is open to anybody with a fast pen or vivid imagination. A new book is coming out on Princess Diana.

For all you Diana fans, get ready for some very unpleasant stuff. Editor Mandy Mersh gives us an insight into what's coming when she says, "If Diana's IQ were five points lower, she would have to be watered daily." Mean stuff, in an age of mean stuff, in a time of tearing down the icons.

It's not just Diana who gets drubbed in death. Others painted with posthumous public scorn include John Lennon and a host of movie stars. Even family members of celebrities write telltale books. It's no surprise Elvis, with all his phobias, is a big target. But really, with Elvis they get more than a little carried away. One book reports Elvis was a consummate masturbator, giving himself pleasure up to seven times a day. How would anyone know that? What does it matter? Or does it just sound okay to people who want to feed on the entrails of the rich and famous? Who can be smart enough, clean enough, not to have half-truths and outright lies written about them? Who can care enough?

No wonder we don't have heroes anymore – or role models. No one can pass the test.

* * *

I have always felt the media needed to more forcefully address the issue of suicide. There was an unwritten rule that we didn't report suicides unless they were obvious, such as a very public plunge from the Macdonald Bridge. By keeping mum on most suicides we were ignoring a serious issue that society needs to address. Family members are usually shocked, devastated and perhaps also embarrassed by the suicide of a loved one. They don't want the act publicized and that is perfectly understandable. Individual deaths would probably not be a news story anyway. The real story is that the number and suicide rates vary from province to province, depending on the year and who is doing the counting. Some figures show Nova Scotia with a slightly lower rate than the national at 11.6 percent per 100,000 people and the New Brunswick rate is slightly higher than the national average at 13.4 percent.

I can't prove it, but I'm willing to bet the actual number is higher than official figures indicate. In all provinces the suicide rate is higher in young men than young women, higher in young people than in seniors and higher in some communities than others. Campbellton, New Brunswick, has a suicide rate of 22.4 percent and Edmundston, New Brunswick, is even higher at 24.9 percent. If those numbers aren't a crisis proportion I don't know what is.

I'm not suggesting we should be insensitive to grieving people, but if every week on a Friday night or in the Saturday papers the number of people who had taken their own lives in the previous week was broadcast or published two things would occur. There would be a new awareness of a serious social problem that has mostly been swept under the carpet, and the suicide rate would decline as a result of the increased attention and concern.

The high rate of suicides in this country is abysmal and I was not one to stay quiet. Here's a commentary from the mid-1990s.

Commentary: Death by our own Hand

It isn't a particularly pleasant subject and no one really likes to talk about it. Except it's touching so many lives these days and the numbers are so mind-boggling we can't keep this deadly issue under wraps any longer. I'm talking about suicide, a subject that has touched so many families in so many countries – but a subject that remains largely taboo.

Last week a report issued the alarming numbers of suicides in France, a big killer among the young. This week the mind-numbing numbers are from Quebec, where suicide is the leading cause of death among Quebec males aged fifteen to forty. More men take their own lives in Quebec than are killed in car accidents or die of heart attacks or succumb to cancer.

The media is discouraged from reporting suicides. We don't tell you of people jumping off the Halifax bridges in the belief it encourages others to do the same. So the subject of suicide remains in the quiet corner of society, whispered about in hushed tones, but not talked about too openly.

The numbers no longer permit us to keep this issue quiet. When taking your own life becomes the number one cause of death, it's time to start talking. Suicide has been under wraps long enough.

* * *

There was plenty of news nationally in the 1990s with our military serving in Somalia as part of a United Nations Humanitarian Effort. Canadians were shocked by grisly photographs of members of the Canadian Airborne Regiment torturing and killing a teenager by the name of Shidane Arone, who they caught sneaking into their compound. It was not the military's finest hour. A video soon surfaced showing other members of the Airborne making racists comments. For a humanitarian exercise they didn't look very humane.

The federal government fumbled the ball, of course. Defense Minister Kim Campbell was trying to replace Brian Mulroney as PC leader and prime minister. She was also facing an upcoming election, but finally the government took the unprecedented step of disbanding the entire regiment. Instead of punishing the guilty parties they punished everyone. And, of course, as we Canadians always do when there's a problem that requires leadership and decision-making, we hold an inquiry.

Commentary: Somalia

Oscar Wilde wrote, "The pure and simple truth is rarely pure and never simple." A fitting signature for the conclusions of the Somalia inquiry. In this case the truth was shielded by cover-up, conspiracy and incredibly bad leadership – both politically and militarily. But the truth often has a way of oozing between the fingers no matter how many hands try to suppress it. Look at the report's conclusions.

Among other things, the commissioners called General Jean Boyle a liar, and General John Dechastelain a poor leader. They said the military establishment in Ottawa either tried to cover up events or just tried to ignore them. They said commanders in Somalia did cover up. They said the military justice system needs reforming. The commissioners said the Chrétien government made things worse by cutting short the inquiry's work.

Instead of digesting this report, evaluating it, appraising it, Canada's new defense minister, who a month ago wouldn't know a tank from a torpedo, is already tearing the report apart – overly critical, he says; no systemic leadership problem, he says. And just to add a pinch of pain to this story, today the *Toronto Star* reports that a legal brief – never made public – has more details about the night a Somali civilian was shot and killed by Canadian soldiers. A soldier, who was given immunity for his evidence, told military police that he and another soldier simultaneously shot the Somali in the back while he was on the ground – not while he was running, as the military claimed.

The plain and simple truth is rarely plain and never simple.

The inquiry was never allowed to completely finish its job. The government wasn't waiting for any more reports and killed it before it had done its work. It did show, however, what was already evident – extremely poor leadership in the military hierarchy. It wasn't so great on the civilian side either.

* * *

I've written many commentaries on the Canadian Senate. Stephen Harper threatens to make drastic changes in this, the biggest of all patronage plums, but getting those old boys (and a few gals too) off their chairs and away from their fat pay cheques and benefits is not an easy task. They're ensconced and unprepared to move any time soon. As of this writing Mr. Harper has not made it happen, even though most people realize the Senate smacks of a cronyism that should belong to past decades and not a modern country.

Canadians should be politically sophisticated and entrenched enough in democratic tradition to feel comfortable to either elect our senators or simply abolish the Senate and send those party hacks and fat asses home. There are repeated calls for substantial changes in our voting system to more accurately reflect the will of the electorate. What better time to improve our total political process? We've done away with the horse and buggy, slavery has disappeared and now the Senate should follow these anachronisms down the sinkhole of history. I dipped way back to find this commentary I wrote in 1978.

Commentary: Axe the Anachronism

Since it appears the federal government isn't planning to do much about inflation, I guess the next best news out of Parliament Hill is the government's intention to reform the House of Commons. It's something long overdue and the Liberals deserve some credit for finally taking the step. The ultimate outcome of this project isn't known, but it should lead to improvements and hopefully speed up the long legislative process now used.

Why, the government's decision to reform the House of Commons has even created a wave in the Senate. It's reported senators have come to life, dusted off the cobwebs and are actually doing something. What they are doing is worrying about their future. The Geritol bunch is concerned about losing its veto power. What they're really worried about is losing their soft jobs in the moldy upper chamber.

There is no bigger anachronism in Canada than the Canadian Senate. Used by successive parties as a dumping ground for party workers and politicians who have run out of steam, the Senate costs money, does little or nothing and has demonstrated for a century we can do without it. Maybe it's time we did. One thing is for sure: either the Senate must be changed to play an integral part in policy-making or it should be abolished. If it plays a primary function in government it seems to me we should start electing senators, making them responsible to the people. One thing is certain. We should do something.

* * *

The senators had nothing to worry about. They still represent the most blatant form of patronage in Canada. Both Brian Mulroney and Pierre Trudeau shamelessly packed the Senate with their cronies, Trudeau as a reward when he was leaving office, Mulroney when he wanted support for his constitutional reform.

John Jay Chapman once wrote, "The world of politics is always twenty years behind the world of thought." I would say that twenty years behind might be acceptable but a century late shouldn't be tolerated.

From time to time the media gets very worked up on the subject of patronage. It is usually the low-level kind where the premier puts his campaign chair in some cushy job they are not qualified to do. It's scandalous and blatant. No one should ever be rewarded with a position they are not qualified to handle. But patronage is necessary at some level in our political system and we will always have it. The only political parties who don't understand that fact are the ones that have never held power and a media that can be terribly naive. The Senate is the highest form of patronage in our political system. Yet irony of ironies, when a new senator is named, the news stories about the appointment seldom contain the word "patronage."

The oddest Senate appointment was that of John Buchanan, the former premier of Nova Scotia. The Buchanan government had simply stayed in power so long it was wilting. As I've said before, no government improves with age and the Buchanan government was tired and sloppy. Corruption was eating around its edges. It had stayed far too long at the trough and had been mired in one scandal after another from that bridge that went nowhere in Cape Breton to high-tech toilet seats, purchased and paid for with taxpayers' money.

When Brian Mulroney offered Buchanan a Senate appointment, the premier literally fled Province House as if he were a man making a jail break. There was only one TV crew standing outside the legislature the very moment he escaped. Buchanan's driver slowed down only long enough for Nova Scotia's longest serving premier to confirm he was through and that all other questions would be handled by somebody else. It was one of the strangest interviews ever given. There was no dignified resignation, no press conference and no official goodbye to the people, just a harried premier and his getaway car.

Long-time MLA and Minister of Agriculture Roger Bacon happened to be deputy premier at the time his boss did a quick exit. Poor Roger suddenly found himself as the man in charge of a dysfunctional government gasping its final breaths. Upon emerging from his first cabinet meeting, Mr. Bacon faced a barrage of questions from reporters waiting outside the cabinet door. To the first question, Premier Bacon replied, "You'll have to ask the premier."

"You are the premier," snapped the reporter.

"Oh, yes," Bacon replied, "I am."

The government was defeated in the next election.

13

Notable People

It's impossible to tell how many newscasts I've read in my career or how many commentaries I've written. Certainly they number in the thousands. The number doesn't matter, but what still does matter is that fascinating aspect of the job. I think I can boil that down to the subjects I covered and the people I wrote about. I wrote about people I had interviewed and people I had never known personally. I've never met Joe DiMaggio but I knew his game and I'd read enough about his life to understand the impact of his hitting streak in 1941. In that year, DiMaggio transcended baseball to become a phenomenon. Maybe it was all about timing but his accomplishment in the ball park took the public's mind off the unpleasant war in Europe. DiMaggio's hitting streak in 56 games brought people who were never interested in baseball to ask, "How'd he do today?" What follows is a commentary from 1999.

Commentary: Goodbye to the Yankee Clipper

Some people might ask why all the fuss about a retired old baseball player. There wasn't such an outpouring of media coverage or sympathy when other greats of the game passed away. When Babe Ruth or Mickey Mantle died, it was big news, but not momentous. While Ruth and Mantle were great ball players, they were not great heroes. Joe DiMaggio was. It's been written we can't all be heroes because someone has got to sit on the curb and clap as they go by. Years after he hung up his glove and put away his bat, people sat on the curb and clapped as Joe DiMaggio went by.

A lot of what's been written about DiMaggio and said about DiMaggio this week seems to miss the mark. Yes, you can put his life in contrast to today's sports figures, but that's it. They are sports figures, not heroes, and there's a big difference between the two. There are many players, but very few heroes. What makes Joe DiMaggio different is he remained a hero all his life and that life wasn't quiet. DiMaggio did the unusual, unheard of things like sitting out several games to demand more money at a time before free agencies or unions. He loved and lost a movie star and wept at her funeral. The life wasn't quiet – the man was. DiMaggio was a player but he mastered the much more difficult role: he was a hero. No wonder his passing is noted with such fanfare.

* * *

David Milgaard owes a lot to his mother. He wouldn't be a free man today without Joyce Milgaard's belief in his innocence and her incredible struggle against the odds to achieve his freedom. In some respects David Milgaard's story follows that of Donald Marshall, another man imprisoned for a crime he didn't commit. Milgaard's freedom followed a convoluted procedure whereby the Supreme Court found him not exactly guilty and not exactly innocent. Eventually, he did receive compensation in 1999 but at the time of this commentary in '97 the wheels of justice were still grinding.

Commentary: The Incarcerated Innocent

Tomorrow we'll know the next chapter in the David Milgaard story. That's when justice officials in Saskatchewan decide whether to hold a new trial or have proceedings stayed. He's already spent more time in penitentiary than most murderers. Another trial would be unreasonable, if not downright inhumane.

But the Milgaard story raises some interesting points. It shows the weaknesses in the criminal justice system, where offenders may pronounce their innocence, but without a strong-willed mother constantly petitioning politicians and whipping up media interest, many cries for a judicial review fall on deaf ears.

Right here in the Maritimes we have Todd Matchett convicted of the robbery and beating death of New Brunswick storekeeper John Glendenning. Matchett says he got bad legal advice and should never have pleaded guilty. The murder, he says, was committed by Alan Legere. Matchett tried to hold a news conference from prison. At first it appeared he'd be allowed to do so, and then suddenly, permission was denied.

What about media access to inmates in penal institutions? Corrections Canada deals with every case individually. There were complaints from several sources, including legal people, to Matchett getting TV attention. In Ottawa, the Federal Justice Department is trying to rewrite the part of the criminal code dealing with retrials.

As for David Milgaard, will he receive compensation for his years in penitentiary? Not necessarily. The Supreme Court didn't find him innocent. It said the continued conviction without the jury hearing fresh evidence would amount to a miscarriage of justice. Not quite innocent, not quite guilty.

Chapter two tomorrow.

* * *

I've always been interested in how time changes our view of events. Voltaire once said, "History is nothing but a pack of tricks we play upon the dead." My question is, in rewriting history are we tricking the dead or the living? Maybe it's just a case of wanting to live with ourselves.

In February of 2008 Manitobans celebrated Louis Riel Day. I wondered what Sir John A. Macdonald would have said. Actually, the gradual recognition of Riel demonstrates how Canadian society has changed. Riel was branded a traitor in his day, condemned to death for murder and hanged by the neck until he was dead. In Riel's day things were either black or white and they remained like that pretty much until the 1960s when society had a fundamental shift. It was more than flower power and free love. We saw the United States become embroiled in a losing war, the Pill gave women more freedom, the church lost its moral authority and its hold on the people. We also discovered there was more than one way to look at an issue. That's just exactly how we've looked at Louis. This is a Final Word I wrote in the late 1990s when Louis Riel's image was already undergoing a cleansing.

Commentary: A Second Chance

The House of Commons is going to honour Louis Riel. It's been more than a hundred years since the federal government hanged him. A hundred years is long enough for historical redemption. The prime minister of the day, John A. Macdonald, was urged to extend leniency to Riel, but the milk of human kindness wasn't in Sir John A.

That day Louis went to the gallows. His crime? Treason. Riel wanted to establish a Métis nation in the west, much like René Lévesque wanted to establish a French nation in Quebec. That's why Riel was hanged. He's being honoured by today's government because his actions contributed to bringing Manitoba into Canada.

The irony is Riel actually established a provisional government at Red River, without federal consent. That could very well be judged an act of treason in itself, but treason is very subjective. Louis Riel will be honoured. Canada! Hanged in one century, honoured in the next, proving once again, this is a nation where you really do receive a second chance.

Garth Turner

Garth Turner has been a Progressive Conservative, an Independent Member of Parliament and a Liberal. He's also a writer and speaker, an investment guru and thinker. I wrote the following commentary in the '90s during one of Turner's job or political transitions. Turner certainly carved out a good career for himself in the investment field. He may have done the same type of work before he became a Member of Parliament, but he wasn't a household name at that time. He was certainly called a few names in Prince Edward Island households and they weren't necessarily complimentary. Turner, in one of his thinking jags, suggested it was high time PEI came to its senses and stopped being a province. Needless to say, I took issue with Mr. Turner.

Commentary: Garth's Garden in the Gulf

Garth Turner is the latest political nonentity to enter the PC leadership race. He no sooner announced he wants to lead Canada than he announced he wants to rewrite the map of Canada. Namely, he wants to abolish Prince Edward Island as a province as a cost-cutting measure.

Imagine, the Cradle of Confederation being demoted to simply a chunk of mud, part of New Brunswick or Nova Scotia. Mr. Turner is from Ontario so naturally his sensitivity to the island may be underdeveloped. If it's just cost-cutting he's interested in, not history, heritage, culture or identity, we could save money by dropping five provinces. We could have one big Atlantic province, Quebec and Ontario could combine, the four western provinces could unite and the entire north could be another province. PEI is part of our past and it may have fewer people than downtown Toronto, but so what?

In the House of Commons, when asked about Mr. Turner's comments, the prime minister said PEI is safe. I guess he means PEI, the Progressive Conservatives and the people of Canada – all safe from Garth Turner. We'll sleep better knowing it.

Joe Clark

I had a pretty good look at Canadian politics over the years, covering political conventions and doing interviews. I watched Brian Mulroney win the Tory leadership and Trudeau say goodbye to the Liberals. I saw Chrétien win and John Turner lose. But nothing stands out like one night in Winnipeg, which wasn't a leadership convention but the annual convention of the Progressive

Conservative Party and a leadership review on the future of Joe Clark.

The Progressive Conservative Party was known for eating their leaders. They did it a few decades earlier to John Diefenbaker and they did it that night to Joe Clark. When the vote on the leadership review was announced, the emotion in the room in Winnipeg Convention Centre was palpable. Clark had told the party he wanted a substantial show of support. He didn't get it. The majority of delegates supported him but not the number he had publicly said was necessary. Clark bravely marched down the centre aisle, passing the thousands of delegates, some applauding, some crying and some cursing. With a wooden smile on his face, Joe Clark shook hands along the way. Hostility and frustration festered in the overheated room.

Reporters are easy targets when people want to lash out and that night people wanted to lash out. One Clark supporter who hung around the fringes of the party in Halifax sneered at me, saying, "I suppose you're happy now." Then he kicked the wall in his pent-up anger.

In the following months, the Conservatives held a leadership convention in which Clark ran and lost to Brian Mulroney. It was anticlimactic compared to that night in Winnipeg when they rejected the guy dubbed Joe Who.

Joe Clark had lost a federal election to the Trudeau Liberals, making his party extremely dissatisfied. He was another one of Canada's politicians who lost an election by telling the truth. He wanted to raise the price of gasoline by eighteen cents a gallon. People were outraged at the idea. Eighteen cents? Imagine! The Liberals felt the public's outrage and fed upon it. They strenuously campaigned against such a steep increase with Pierre Trudeau claiming it would be hard on consumers and business too. When Trudeau won the election and came to power, the price of gasoline far surpassed the eighteen-cent increase proposed by Joe Clark.

In politics broken promises aren't unusual. In Canadian politics they are recurring themes. Joe Clark was a contradiction to the old adage "honesty pays." It didn't for him.

Commentary: In Politics You Can Keep a Good Man Down

The story is all over the media today. Joe Clark will announce this weekend he's leaving politics. His twenty-one years in public life included a few months as prime minister and seven stormy years as Opposition leader when his party often acted like he was the enemy.

In the early 1970s I worked in Calgary as a television reporter. In those days a very junior MP used to deliver party press releases. I never guessed that junior Member of Parliament would one day become party leader and prime minister.

The real tragedy of Joe Clark was that he tried to level with the Canadian public during the federal election of 1980. In his straightforward style, he told voters he would raise the price of gasoline by eighteen cents a gallon. He lost; the Liberals won and raised the price of gasoline three times higher than Clark had promised. The man who used to be known as Joe Who will walk away from the cabinet immediately and politics totally this summer.

Joe Clark never really had the opportunity to prove himself as prime minister. His loss, and maybe ours as well.

Roy Rogers

I was in the newsroom the day Roy Rogers died in 1998 and an entire era of my life instantly replayed in my mind. When I was a kid in the 1950s, Roy Rogers was King of the Cowboys with the most recognizable face in America. I actually remember two guys in a fist fight over who was best, Roy Rogers or Gene Autry. We took our boyhood heroes seriously back then. This was a guy every boy wanted to be like. He fought the bad fellows and always won. He rode a horse, carried a lasso and wore a cowboy hat. Every kid knew the name of Roy's horse, his wife's horse and his sidekick's horse. It was a time before television and we were surrounded by American comic book culture. Roy Rogers was part of that era. His photo graced the cover of numerous comics, he sang on the radio and he made movies. When he died in 1998 the only thing I could do for Roy was pay my final respects.

Commentary: King of the Cowboys

He didn't exactly slip away unnoticed, but considering how big he was fifty years ago, the death of Roy Rogers was a rather quiet affair. A short slot in the news, a video of Roy with Dale, an old movie clip with Gabby Hayes or a photo of Roy standing by a stuffed Trigger as if he's ready to mount that old horse one more time and ride off into the sunset.

The death of Roy Rogers is more than just the passing of another dime store cowboy. Roy Rogers was much more than that. He was a true American icon, a symbol of a time when heroes wore white hats.

We didn't wear white hats in Parrsboro where I rode the range as a youth, but I remember two hombres squaring off in the school yard. Fisticuffs, earnest punches from scrawny arms over who was best – Roy Rogers or Gene Autry. Now such things are called disturbances that require counselling. We just called them fights. Roy fought but never killed – hardly ever drew his gun. In one movie, he took on four guys, a real donnybrook. Got his hat knocked off and just a little trickle of blood at the corner of his mouth, just a spot. The other guys – every one out cold.

It sounds pretty hokey now when there are no heroes, just the Bruce Willis type, blowing off heads with a high-powered handgun. Today's people on the screen somehow don't deserve the adoration given Roy Rogers. Heroes died with Vietnam, went up in smoke with Woodstock, went down with Watergate.

The death of Roy Rogers just reminds us it's final. Guys in white hats wouldn't be riding back. They've gone off into the sunset and taken that age of innocence with them.

R.B. Bennett

A number of Canada's prime ministers have died while out of the country. Thompson, Tupper and Bennett all died in England and in the late 1990s, some fifty-one years after he died in his bathtub, a group worked to bring R.B.'s bones back to Canada. They actually wanted to establish a Bennett museum and some people thought bringing back the bones would, well, make the museum more authentic. Following is a commentary I wrote in 1998.

Commentary: Bennett's Bones

I don't know what you think of moving dead prime ministers around but there is a move afloat to bring R.B. Bennett back to Canada. Richard Bedford Bennett was Canada's eleventh prime minister and they want to dig him up in England and move him to New Brunswick, around the Hopewell Cape area where he was born. Then they want to start an R.B. Bennett museum. This may be taking tourist attractions too far. And would R.B. Bennett be an attraction anyway? He wasn't in life. Has fifty years in the grave made him somehow more appealing?

R.B. Bennett is buried in England, where he escaped to after five years as prime minister of Canada. Bennett was blamed for the Depression. He didn't deserve all the blame, but he wasn't totally guiltless. As Gordon Donaldson points out in his 1997 book, The Prime Ministers of Canada, Bennett was aloof and left the impression of a misguided prig, an arch-conservative who hoarded the public's money when the public wanted and needed it. He was a one-man show: prime minister while holding the finance and external affairs portfolios. The old story goes that once, when seen talking to himself, someone asked, "What's he doing?" and someone answered, "He's holding a cabinet meeting."

R.B. Bennett seemed out of touch with the suffering during the Depression. Once during that despair faced by millions came his Prime Minister's Thanksgiving message, cabled from England. Canadians, he cabled, should be especially thankful for the manifold blessings that providence has bestowed on them.

R.B. Bennett left Canada because he didn't want to be here. We should continue to comply with his wishes.

The Queen Mother

My wife Helen and I were standing near Buckingham Palace in August of 2001 when the Queen Mother, celebrating her one hundred and first birthday, made a short public appearance. She was accompanied by members of the Royal Family including Princess Margaret, who looked older than her mother and died a short time later. Unlike Margaret, the Queen Mum aged well. Even at 101 she had that enduring charm that she carried throughout her life. And what a remarkable life it was.

She rose to the responsibility thrust upon her and her husband's shoulders. She had hardly settled into being queen when the war started. She was a tower of strength during the German blitz of English cities, refusing to leave London for the safety of Canada. Her words were, "The children could not go without me, I could not possibly leave the King, and the King would never go." She was aristocracy, of course, a product of the British class system. After Buckingham Palace was bombed in September of 1940, she confided she was glad the palace had been bombed because she could now look the East End in the face.

I met the Queen Mother during one of her Canadian visits. She politely asked me to keep my television camera off her while she ate and I complied. I am not a great monarchist but I do admire the Queen Mum.

Commentary: Good Queen Mum

These are turbulent times for the Royal Family. Rumours and reckless reporting often take a small truth and turn it into a big lie. The stress of the constant spotlight on young members of the monarchy can produce tortured private lives.

But there is one member of the monarchy who has always stood head and shoulders above it all. She has been an example of dignity and strength through every adversity life has thrown at her. She was there when Hitler's bombs were blowing up British cities and she's been there in times of peace.

If you have ever read Sarah Bradford's book *The Reluctant King: The Life and Reign of George VI 1895-1952*, you will know the book tells in great detail of the abdication of Edward VIII and gives us a better understanding of how, as two lesser members of the monarchy, she and her husband were thrown into the public limelight much against their will.

I'm talking, of course, about that remarkable lady known as The Queen Mother. She is ninety-two today and whether you are a fan of the Royal Family or not, this woman deserves respect for the life she has led and the sacrifices she has made in youth and in old age. A remarkable life, a remarkable woman.

René Lévesque

Atlantic premiers and New England governors get together every year to discuss matters of mutual interest. Despite the fact they've been meeting for years they haven't made much headway in many areas and events such as the heightened fear of terrorists have overtaken them. I don't know if they still invite Quebec to these meetings but they used to, and René Lévesque was premier one year when I covered the conference in New Hampshire. Lévesque took strong exception to a question I asked at a news conference after one of the sessions. The issue was Quebec's plans to take over auto insurance and I inquired if Quebec insurance policies would be honoured elsewhere if Quebec separated from Canada. Well! You'd think I told him I'd slept with his mother. Lévesque danced around the room glaring at me while issuing a continuous monologue about the sanctity and reputation of Quebec that would be upheld when it was a free and independent country.

The American reporters watched this thin little guy with fire in his eyes in a stunned silence. René Lévesque was a great showman and he dazzled the U.S. media with his passion and the flame in his eyes as he waltzed around the room glowering at me and talking with his hands. They wondered if all Canadian politicians were like this. Ask a tough question and you get a twenty-minute dressing down from the man. There were strange stories coming out of Canada at the time. In what other country did the prime minister's wife run off with a rock band (The Rolling Stones) and a goodly portion of the population try to sever ties with the rest of the nation? This is a commentary I wrote after my assignment in New Hampshire in 1978.

Commentary: The Edge of Canada

During a visit to the United States recently a U.S. reporter told me how lucky I was to live in Canada because we have such interesting people in politics. They have straitlaced Jimmy Carter and his beer-drinking brother Billy, who receives more publicity than the president. We have the likes of René Lévesque and, of course, the Trudeaus. Far more interesting and in Canada no less!

We take it all in stride. Can you imagine the reaction in the United States if Rosalynn Carter ran off with a rock band, left her husband to make movies and write a very personal book? Only in Canada, you say ... quite true.

Well, Canada's best known couple is back in the news today. There are stories from staff members of the Vancouver Sun which claim Pierre and Margaret Trudeau will soon be back together. The stories are that the Trudeaus will reaffirm their marriage vows in Vancouver at Christmas and the prime minister will resign the next week. This comes from two of Canada's best known reporters with plenty of connections on the west coast, where Mrs. Trudeau's parents reside.

But that doesn't mean the stories are true. A better indication is the reaction from the Prime Minister's Office, which described the report as unadulterated rubbish. That reaction makes me wonder if indeed the stories are correct. The timing is absolutely perfect. Pierre has just given an interview on marriage ... something he seldom does. He says the key to marriage is maturity and that's why he didn't marry until late in life. And, of course, there's Margaret's book ... so sensitive the publisher is keeping a tight lid on security.

To promote sales, however, we do learn Margaret does relate in frank and candid detail her extramarital relationships. Oh, the suspense of it all.

Will Pierre and Margaret get back together?

Will Pierre read the book?

Will Pierre and Margaret separate once more?

Will Pierre discover maturity?

Will Pierre resign the leadership?

Will Margaret give up her movie career?

Will Pierre buy the *Vancouver Sun*?

Tune in tomorrow for another chapter of The Edge of Canada … a half true story of real people.

Somehow, Jimmy Carter's beer-drinking brother is beginning to look better all the time.

14

Words and Names

Samuel Johnson wrote, "Words are like money: there is nothing so useless, except when put to use."

Very often in today's society, words are substituted for serious thought leading to decisive action. We're overrun with verbal pomposity and politically correct terminology. In today's complex society we have the media that feeds on words and bureaucracy that feeds off the media.

I've always despised inflated language and the need to make things sound greater than they actually are. When a young girl dies tragically, the media reports the entire community is in shock. No, it isn't. That's the type of exaggeration that slides into media talk more and more frequently. Maybe the media wants the entire community to be in shock and thus states a situation that isn't so. The community is whirling. Is it? Show me the whirl.

We fancy things up with what we consider high-powered names. Institutions such as hospitals must be named by committee. When the Queen Elizabeth II Health Sciences Centre opened its doors to the public, newsrooms were given directions on how to properly use the name. There was a full page of do's and don'ts. Under the heading "Please Use" were the words Queen Elizabeth II Health Sciences Centre. Under "Please Avoid" were Queen Elizabeth Hospital, QE II Hospital, Queen E II and Queen E 2.

We were instructed to call the Halifax Infirmary, the Halifax Infirmary Site, not the Halifax Infirmary. We were told to avoid calling the Victoria General the VG. And so on. The only problem with such instructions, dear, nefarious naming committee, is that real people don't talk like that! People converse verbally or text in the manner they speak. They don't talk like mandarins who have been stuffed with government press releases.

The eradication of masculine words from our language may in some cases be legitimate but sometimes it is just plain silly, such as the direction I received from my company in 1996 that the word "fisherman" would in the future in all news copy be changed to "fisher."

This was just an opportunity to have some fun, and I didn't even mind taking a shot at my own employer for being so damn silly and following the herd of political correctness.

Commentary: Fishers are Furry and Always Have Been.

The term "The Powers That Be" is a peanut butter phrase that can be spread over almost anything.

In this company, The Powers That Be sent us all a memo the other day declaring that from now on in news reports, the word "fisherman" will be replaced by the word "fisher." Now, I don't want to get in a public dispute with the people I work for – that's usually not wise, but I think they should understand something. Almost all fishermen hate the word fisher. And secondly, a fisher is a member of the weasel family, a furry little critter that scurries around Maritime woodlands.

I have a personal interest in this. The time may come when I cover one of those fiery demonstrations fishermen are prone to these days. I'd just as soon not be the guy who called them furry little weasels. If you get my drift.

Weasels aren't skunks, but they still don't smell very good and neither does this directive from head office. I'm all in favour of making the language gender inclusive but really! Fishermen are fishermen – and if a woman works alongside them, she's a fisherman too. Reducing them to furry little weasels is a definite demotion.

The Powers That Be are fishing off the wrong wharf and all they've caught so far is a really dumb idea!

Proper Names

Of course, this brought forth several letters. Most people agreed with me but one writer took me to task for calling those people in New Brunswick furry, smelly little animals. Today the word fisher is commonly used, except, of course, by fishermen who think the whole thing is a bunch of bullshit.

I always refer to the amalgamation of Halifax and area as the death of Dartmouth as the name Dartmouth has virtually disappeared. At the time of writing this commentary in 1998, Bedford was making noises about regaining its identity. Go for it, Bedford. Amalgamation gave me the opportunity to get away from harder news for a night to have some fun with proper names.

Commentary: Name Game

Reg Rankin has one of those alliterative names like Robert Redford. With a name like that he could be an actor or country music star. Here's Reg Rankin with number twenty on the hit parade.

Reg Rankin is, in fact, a Halifax municipal councillor in the Halifax Regional Municipality – better known as the HRM. Sounds like some bowel disease, doesn't it? *He's got HRM – only months to live.*

Anyway, HRM is the product of amalgamating Halifax, Dartmouth, Bedford and all other outlying communities under one big government. It was supposed to be a cost-saving move but the municipality is $12 to $14 million in debt and water bills and taxes may go sky-high. All of this aside, Mr. Rankin says Halifax Regional Municipality is too long a name. Why not just Halifax? HRM is now on signs, city vehicles and stationary. Despite the cost of changing things again, what about Dartmouth, the City of Flakes, and Bedford? Are these communities just to disappear by naming the new unimproved supercity simply Halifax? Excuse me, but Dartmouthians, Bedfordtonians, Waveronians and Sackvillians – it's time for you to speak or lose the identity of your community. The Robert Redfords of the world are ready to cast the name of your town into amalgamated oblivion.

It's only fair if old names are going, they should all go. If you want to wipe the history slate clean, come up with a new name, incorporating at least the communities of Dartmouth, Bedford and Sackville as well as Halifax. How about Halmouthford, Dartiford or Sackifax.

Sure, you think the heat's got me, I've finally flipped. I know they take a little getting used to. Just say them a few times. Sackifax actually grows on you as does Halmouthford, or Dartiford. They almost roll right off the tongue after a few hours.

We took our news cameras to the street of HRM yesterday to ask citizens their opinion. They don't care. If we listen to them we should just call it Hellwithit. Sackifax, Halmouthford, Dartiford, Bedifax, Reg Rankin, Robert Redford – I've got to go now. I think I've got HRM.

* * *

Of course, political correctness always has its goofy edge. Those who wished to eradicate everything male from our vocabulary got carried away in their enthusiasm, never more so when it came to the word "manhole."

Commentary: Everybody's Hole

It's always delightful when things don't conform to the wretched policies of political correctness. Those who eradicate church hymns and destroy the most beautiful literature in the Bible have been – I'm sorry to say – successful. The Twenty-Third Psalm is a good example.

He maketh me to lie down in green pastures.

Presently that line says something about being in the green as if you're making a trip to the salad bar or your nearest ATM to get cash.

Thank goodness there are certain words that resist this corset of correctness and I love them. The best word may be manhole. So far it has refused to die. It won't go away. People hole is awkward, utility hole isn't catching on and woman hole – no way!

The politically correct gang are turning a fisherman into a fisher and a chairman into a chair but so far they've failed with manhole. It isn't so much about men, just a hole in the ground with a top on it, but at least it's resistant and in this world of spineless compliance, that's something.

* * *

The best person to mangle the language was Yogi Berra, the New York Yankees venerable catcher. When he made it into *Bartlett's Familiar Quotations*, I just had to salute him for the mangled joy he's given all of us.

Commentary: Quoting Yogi

Yogi Berra reached another plateau this week. John Bartlett started his long-standing reference books, *Bartlett's Familiar Quotations*, back in 1855. The 16th edition has just been released and that most quotable man, Yogi Berra, has finally made it. Yogi may not have said everything attributed to him, but he said enough to be a living legend of fractured language. The best known Yogi-ism is his famous, "It ain't over till it's over." Another great Yogi quotation is his theory of life which goes, "When you come to a fork in the road, take it." How about Yogi's observation on observation? "You can observe a lot by watching."

My favourite Yogi story takes place on a very hot New York summer day, one of those humid, oppressive August afternoons. New York mayor John Lindsey and his wife were hosting a Sunday brunch for the Yankees. Yogi showed up wearing a lime green suit. Mrs. Lindsey welcomed him with the words, "Why, Yogi, you look nice and cool in that suit."

To which Yogi replies, "Thanks, Mrs. Lindsey, you don't look so hot yourself."

May not be Shakespeare, but it sure is fun.

* * *

There are some wonderful stories about words and how, at times, they live after us. Take, for example, the wish of Long Wolf and his words that were acted upon long after his death by a woman who never knew him, but who fulfilled his wish anyway.

Commentary: The Wish of Long Wolf

Last weekend both Halifax and Saint John hosted events dealing with books. In Halifax it was Word on the Street and in Saint John it was A Writer's Workshop.

This week in Nova Scotia, the Governor General raised the flag on a First Nation ceremony in Halifax.

I mention these events because in another part of the world, there is a story that deals with both books and First People. It was a secondhand book, actually, read by a housewife in Worcestershire, England. It was the story of the life and death of Long Wolf, a Sioux warrior who died of pneumonia while performing in London with Buffalo Bill's Wild West Show in 1892.

Long Wolf wanted to be buried in his native South Dakota. Travel was slow back then and his wife worried the body would be dumped overboard if she pressed for a final cruise for her dead husband. So he was buried in a cemetery in central London.

The reader of the secondhand book was Elizabeth Knight. She read the story – and did more.

She went to the cemetery and found the neglected grave. She didn't stop there. She wrote to a newspaper in South Dakota. Eventually, the granddaughter of Long Wolf was tracked down and six years after Elizabeth Knight opened that secondhand book, the body of Long Wolf is being flown home. His last wish finally granted, 105 years after his death.

All because a lady in England read a book and added a chapter to the story under her own personal initiative.

* * *

English is a living language and in today's world media literacy is extremely important. Never believe anything you see or hear without filtering it through your own intelligence. The military has plenty of buzz words. Such terms as "collateral damage" and "friendly fire" are oxymoronic terms that instill more insensitivity than understanding. The media uses a lot of words without thinking about the actual meaning or possible redundancy. Perhaps the most prominent today is "went missing" for "disappeared." A few others are: sunny skies (skies are clear but never sunny); a deliberately set arson fire; an unforeseen tragedy.

Words build us up or destroy us so we must be very careful how we use them. As Romantic poet Percy Bysshe Shelley wrote, "He gave man speech, and speech created thought, which is the measure of the Universe."

15

Lighter Bits

The great joy of journalism is the variety of the job. I'd be interviewing a farmer on Monday, a fisherman on Tuesday, a musician on Wednesday, a cabinet minister Thursday and when I woke up Friday morning I just never knew who would be making news that day or what I'd be doing. It wasn't just interviews but the entire range of stories that made up the day's program. Producers described the hour-long six o'clock news as The Black Hole, a bottomless pit that has to be filled each day with hard news, weather, interviews and what was known as fluffy features.

As a commentator I could write on any subject: local, national or international. I could use any item that caught my interest or captured my attention. And I would travel the entire range of topics from the hard, heartbreaking stories of tainted blood to tainted tuna, from Somalia to the Prime Minister's Office and those quirky human interest pieces. The hard news stories more readily tarnish in the distant light. People stories have weathered the years better than newsy material. When it comes to human interest or humour, some stories just stand the test of time. Here are a few examples.

I've always enjoyed sightings of the Virgin Mary, which occur more frequently than you might expect. Some of the sightings are right here in the Maritimes. Nobody really knows why but '98 was a good year for sightings of all kinds. The Virgin had a habit of popping up where least expected, from a Cape Breton coffee shop to a billboard in Albert County, New Brunswick. You just never knew where there might be a sighting. This one was in November of 1998.

Commentary: A Virgin in New Brunswick

Plenty of news relating to God this week.

While folks in Albert County, New Brunswick, watched the outline of the Virgin Mary on a billboard this week, archeologists have pinpointed the exact location of the Garden of Eden in a fertile valley near the border between Iran and Iraq: a valley full of greenery, fruit, and fig trees and, of course – snakes.

While these things are going on, a microbiologist, Dr. Leoncio Garza-Valdes, has come out with a new book called The DNA of God. You see, carbon testing in the 1980s pretty well proved the Shroud of Turin dated from the twelfth or thirteenth century. Not so fast, says this scientist. At the University of Texas, Garza-Valdes's examination of the shroud shows the garment is covered with a visible bioplastic coating of bacteria and fungus that he and colleagues suspect developed over centuries and screwed up the carbon testing.

The microbiologists also report that what was thought to be red paint or dye on the shroud is actually blood – blood that their tests confirm contains X and Y chromosomes, making it human blood, and that it is the most common type among Jewish men. Garza-Valdes believes it's the blood of Jesus. One reason he is so certain is that they found a tiny piece of wood in the blood. The wood is oak, common in Jerusalem.

And you know the question they were asked that would have been inconceivable a few years ago. The question is – by taking the DNA from the blood, could they clone Jesus? The answer is no. The blood is too degraded, at least for today's science. What about tomorrow?

* * *

Makes an obscure image on a billboard seem very primitive, doesn't it?

Only Christ himself could outrank the Virgin Mary and leave it to Cape Bretoners to have the upper hand. They claimed an image of the Savior himself; you could see it at Tim Hortons.

Having said what I did in my commentary, I must add that the blood type on the shroud was AB negative, which belongs to only 3.2 percent of the world's people and the highest percentage of these live in northern Palestine.

Commentary: Coffee and Christ

It is the strangest story we've had in a long time. Not so much that people saw the face of Christ on the side of a Tim Hortons donut shop – but that the owners didn't want it there. They changed the lights and the image disappeared. It's so different from what you might expect. If it happened in the United States, they'd be promoting it, charging a fee and organizing lectures at the site, selling brochures and trinkets.

While they were seeing Christ in beautiful Bras d'Or, other things are happening in Cape Breton. The government is promising to put more effort into creating a better cash flow. The Municipality of Sydney is staggering under a debt of $630,000. Toxic goop remains behind Frederick Street. The cancer rate is the highest in Canada and Tim Hortons decides whatever is on the side of its building had better prove itself. If it's still there after we change the lighting – well, that's different, isn't it?

There are a lot of jokes, of course, spread as much by Cape Bretoners as any other group. It goes like this – if the Lord was going to visit Canada and wanted to take a coffee break, of course he'd go to Cape Breton. It's tough making a go of life in Cape Breton. Even images – holy or unholy – won't be taken seriously unless they pass a change of lighting test. You have to give those people at Tim Hortons their due. They'll never be accused of capitalizing on the faith or folly of others.

* * *

Sometimes when scanning the news wires in search of a subject for The Final Word, I'd come across some emotionally touching story that I just had to pass along. I knew my viewers wanted more than the everyday news fare. They wanted a variety of subjects, something they could talk about the next day, such as this story.

Commentary: He Cares for Me

Instead of the cod crisis in Newfoundland or the war in Sarajevo, I thought I'd leave you tonight with one of those wonderful stories that comes across my desk every now and then.

A construction crew in the United States was putting a road through a rural area, knocking down trees. As the work progressed, a superintendent noticed that one tree had a nest of baby birds too young to fly. He marked that tree so it wouldn't be knocked down.

Several weeks later the fledglings had learned to fly and were gone. The superintendent ordered the tree cut down. As it crashed to the ground, the nest fell clear and some the material that the birds had gathered to make the nest scattered to the ground. Part of it was a scrap of paper from a Sunday school pamphlet. On the paper were the words "He cares for me."

* * *

I continued to dabble in bad poetry in my commentaries right up to my final night on the air. In a week with horrendous news it was just a way to break away from the blood and gore and the indignities we humans managed to inflict on one another. When the venerable British firm of Marks & Spencer closed their only store in metro Halifax-Dartmouth it was time to put the event in rhyme.

Commentary: Cheerio From Us

So there goes Marks & Spencer. The traditional British chain is pulling out of Canada. It is a sad night for the St. Andrew's Society. The news brought forth this ditty for a Friday evening.

"The time has come," Mr. Marks said,
"To speak of other things:
Of leaving here and closing shop, of pushing off and going,
There's no big profit here, besides it's very often snowing."
Mr. Spencer gave a sigh and said, "It is so very true.

It gives me pain to say goodbye but what are we to do.
Our tweedy wools and linen shirts don't seem to fit the bill.
Our canned cookies sit on the shelf, it is a bitter pill."
So Mr. Marks and Mr. Spencer drew up a proclamation.
They posted it far and wide without a moment's hesitation.
"Dear Canada, we bid you ta and cheerio from us.
We're packing up our kippers and leaving without a fuss.
The quality we've got it, to our goods we give a cheer.
But we have to say, old boy, it's tally-ho from here.
Sorry for our clerks, they were the very best.
But there is just so much before the upper lip begins to crest.
If you're across the pond, drop in for a spot of tea.
Just ask for Spencer or, Mr. Marks – that's me."

And so, the retail landscape changes. Marks & Spencer leave and those who want fine British goods are simply left to grieve.

* * *

There isn't a volunteer organization in the world that isn't trying to raise money for their cause. I've been involved in many fundraisers and some work better than others. Some just don't work at all.

Commentary: Kiss Me Pig

The strangest story of the week may be out of Indiana, where organizers of a local fair wanted to raise money by setting up a pig-kissing booth. Now, I wouldn't think there would be a big lineup to kiss a pig, even for a good cause. We Maritimers have a ceremony called Kissing the Cod and look what's happened to the cod – all but disappeared.

Let's face it, kissing critters isn't healthy. It's bad for the animals and the pig farmers of Indiana were quick to point that out. One farmer refused to let his pigs get involved, saying a kissed pig could get a strep infection. Besides, pigs get stressed in such situations – forced to kiss puckered-up humans smelling of perspiration or perfume.

At least the cod are usually dead! But live, squalling, sensitive little pigs, you can almost hear them plead, "Put me back in the trough."

At last report, the pig-kissing contest had been cancelled. Chalk one up for the pigs in the ongoing struggle between those animals on four legs and those animals on two.

* * *

While we're on the subject of high comedy, the '60s and '70s saw the emergence of provincial law reform commissions. These groups started the work of recommending the updating and deleting of various antiquated laws that bogged down legal books. Some funny laws and some weird cases were uncovered. This commentary was written in 1978.

Commentary: Silly Laws

It's true. There are times you could look at Canadian laws and cry – or laugh, depending on your frame of mind. This story happened some time ago but came to light again last week.

A man was riding his horse through a Toronto park. Because he was poor he had sold his saddle and was using a feather pillow instead. But on this fateful day the horse fell and broke its leg and the man had to shoot the horse to put it out of its considerable misery. Later the man was charged with violating the Small Bird Act. He was fined $200 for killing a bird. The bird – in case you're not following this – was the horse.

According to the magistrate, who must have been a real winner, the law defines a bird as an animal with two legs covered with feathers. The horse was covered with a feather pillow. The fact the horse had four legs instead of two didn't bother the magistrate, who ruled the law meant at least two legs.

The man was convicted, which raises the question: if a man covers another man in feathers then shoots him, under Canadian law, has the man committed a murder or violated the Small Bird Act? Think about it.

16

Leaving

By the end of 1996, I had had enough. Although I despaired over the numbing boredom of what our news programming had become, that was not the real reason I decided to leave broadcasting. The fact was, I really hadn't fallen out of love with television as much as I'd fallen in love with something else – writing.

I noticed when working on a five-part series where I was both writing and producing that I was enjoying the writing more than the producing. I could put myself away from the newsroom and write in quiet and be quite happy. Besides, I had an idea for a book. It was the story of a young boy and his father, which would become *The Parrsboro Boxing Club*.

An idea formed. A plan hatched that, if successful, would give me an income and let me write something besides television scripts. Finally, when the timing was right I approached management with a proposal that I was certain they would accept if I coached my words in just the right way, and believe me, by then I knew the right words.

"I have a plan that can save you some money."

That was the way I put it to Slick Rick, the Global manager. I was prepared to take a cut in pay in exchange for a reduction in my working hours. I would continue to read the major newscast and write The Final Word. I would have mornings and some of the afternoons free to work on my book. I would arrive at the station at 3 p.m. and leave at 7 p.m.

In proposing such a change I realized I was also designing my own exit from the company because my status would change from full-time to part-time. It would be a gradual exit and an opportunity to begin a writing career.

That arrangement worked for a year. Then I signed a contract to do commentaries only for two more years. I finished my broadcasting career at the end of June 2000 and after thirty-nine years, I walked away as happy to be going out as I was coming in.

I've remained that way. I miss the give and take with the audience but haven't missed television. I've written five books, travelled, done some documentary work and even had bit parts in a few movies. Plus the craziest thing I've ever done, taken a shot at politics.

My short but fun-filled political career began one quiet afternoon when I was putting the finishing touches to my second novel, Dream of the Dove. There had been a lot of research, and the work had been intense. I was ready to get out of my chair and try something totally different. At that very moment when I was thinking such thoughts, the phone rang. It was Russell McKinnon from Cape Breton. Russell was a sitting Liberal MLA and had been a cabinet minister in the Savage government. He asked me almost immediately if I would be interested in going into politics. In fact, would I care to run for the Nova Scotia Liberal leadership?

There was no question they wanted more names in the race just to whip up a little excitement. Danny Graham had just withdrawn his name, which further depleted the short list of candidates. I knew all this and if it had been any other time in my life I would have declined immediately. But with two books under my belt I was ready for new and challenging things.

The Liberals needed an infusion of new ideas. Their traditional political landscape had been usurped by the New Democrats. After John Savage and the infighting, they were in disarray. My background in politics had been as an observer but that isn't such a bad background if you're really interested. I'd covered every political convention federally and provincially since the 1960s. I'd seen leaders up close and I had some original ideas about politics.

Russell arranged some meetings for me with party organizers in Halifax. My big concern was twofold. I had been a commentator and had not always been easy on the Liberals. My other concern was lack of history in the party, particularly in Cape Breton, where the Liberals had most of their strength but I wouldn't have any base at all. That was no problem, said Russell with enthusiasm. He was a Cape Breton member of the legislature and he had plenty of support.

So, after a couple of weeks of reflection and conversations and knowing it was the biggest long shot of my life, I said yes. Then Danny Graham jumped back in the race and Russell, my recruiter, informed me he could no longer support my candidacy. The long shot had just become longer. I thought about getting out, since my Cape Breton support had already crumbled before the race really began. But no, I had ideas, innovative, fresh ideas and what did I have to lose? I was in a race with no solid block of support except Cumberland and West Hants. Both great places, but with a scarcity of Liberals.

On the plus side, I had a very dedicated group of supporters and of all the four candidates I know we had the most enjoyable campaign. I filled the Liberal debates with new ideas that went absolutely nowhere. I talked of taking the party back to its grass roots and establishing a system to give ordinary people more say in policy-making; I charged that decision-making had been locked away behind closed doors long enough. Whatever I was selling, the Liberals weren't buying.

The race was filled with skullduggery too. Accusations hit the media concerning the rigging of the memberships. The Liberals decided to investigate the accusations themselves, rather than call in the police. The media ran stories but didn't investigate. Of course, the Liberal investigation found nothing and went nowhere.

As expected, I lost badly. Some said I was too old or too radical or I had slapped the party publicly too many times on television. My wife Helen was immensely relieved.

When the race was over Bruce Stephen, my campaign chairman, and I had a meeting with Mike Savage, the president of the Nova Scotia Liberal Party, to see about having our $10,000 deposit refunded. It wasn't my money, but it was raised by supporters and I wanted them to get it back instead of being pocketed by the party. The Liberals were ambiguous about the rules on candidate's deposits – bending the rules at times to give the money back if the candidate ran a worthy campaign and refusing a refund in other instances. Mike Savage promised to investigate the issue and get back to us. Six years later I'm still waiting.

In the end, I was as disillusioned with the Liberals as I had been with CanWest. But in any event it had all worked out wonderfully. I went back to writing. The Liberals are on their third leader since my leadership run and I still don't know what they stand for. But frankly, these days I'm not eagerly trying to find out.

It had been another life experience. I made many friends and met some very good people. All taken together – broadcasting, politics and writing – it's been a marvelous time.

When it was announced I was leaving television one lady wrote me a very touching letter. When my commentaries weren't on television her budgie refused to sing. What more could a guy ask for?

Commentary: One for the Bird

For those who follow this program on a regular basis, it's not news that I've been away for most of the summer pursuing other projects, and it's nice to know that some people missed this commentary and for that I say thank you.

Perhaps the strangest story concerning my absence comes from a woman who lives near Windsor. She told me her budgie watched The Final Word every night. As the short opening theme came on the air, the bird would move along its perch, cock its head at a proper angle and listen for the full moment. In July, when I wasn't there, the bird followed the same procedure. It would move along its perch and wait. It waited and waited in vain, day in and day out. One night it keeled over and dropped dead.

"I'm convinced, Mr. Graham," she told me, "my bird died because you weren't on the air."

Now, I can just imagine smirks out there, the guffaws, and the sneering jealousy of newspaper people whose only connection with birds is when their columns line the bottom of cages and are gradually covered with excrement. I know many viewers might say this is for the birds, but this is a free country and that lady and me, we can believe what we want to. And I say the budgie died for lack of commentary. That's her story and my story, and we're sticking to it!

17

News Award Graveyard

One of the most unsettling experiences concerning Global/MITV happened after I left the company. I was invited back for an interview on my second novel, *Dream of the Dove*. I hadn't been in the building for a couple of years and the experience gave me a weird feeling as I walked down the halls. The place had changed. There were fewer people around and the atmosphere seemed even more doleful.

The one thing that remained constant was the pleasant smile of Duane Lowe. I always said Duane was the hardest working employee in the place. She did about three jobs, producing almost single-handedly an hour-long show five days a week, lining up guests, researching interview subjects, plus making public relations appearances. Despite the workload, she was seldom flustered and handled everyone with a genuine gracefulness. We did a good interview and I had an opportunity to show my book on air, which is all you can ask.

When I was leaving, one of the original studio people, a guy who had been there from the start and who will remain nameless for his own protection, took me aside. He wanted to show me something in the storage area at the back of the building. We went upstairs to a loft above the carpentry shop where sets and old furniture were stored. There, resting on several tables and desks, were all the news, documentary and programming awards won by MITV over the past ten years.

That was the other change that made the station so somber and empty-looking. In the transition to CanWest/Global, they had stripped the walls of all mention of MITV. Instead of celebrating the company's past, they were burying it. Looking at the awards hidden away yet lovingly displayed brought back a flood of memories. The years spun by. I was shaken by the sight of all that effort and work laid out like corpses on a table. Even our national news award for the documentary *Proud People of Our Coast* lay there. Every award held some memory for me, even the ones I had nothing to do with, such as the one Stan and Wendy Johnson won in 1988, the first year MITV was on the air, for their children's program called *Something Else* – a program eventually sold to a network in the United States.

I was touched by the tenderness and caring of the original MITV studio staff, who had set up an almost secret shrine to the by-gone days. I was told to take what I wanted because the framed prizes and scripted plaques were probably headed for the dumpster. I took one of the mementos and left the rest for others who had contributed as much or more than me. But the experience shook me. Television is so transitory, just a flicker of light on a screen. The best story you might ever do in your life is gone in a minute and a half. Awards give you that hard memory to hang onto. Back in 1988, when we started, I was so proud of MITV. I felt we would eventually overcome the incredible hindrance of not reaching more than a handful of people. We held such promise for local news and innovative programming. The efforts of so many people were being discarded and somehow it made me sad.

Actually, my emotions were mixed. I walked away from Global Television rather depressed about the past but buoyant about the future. I was free of television deadlines, daily makeup, ridiculous memos and the discipline of feigning interest in irrelevant stories. Although I had been gone from television for a few years, it was on that day that I felt a certain separation from the business that at first I could not identify. It certainly wasn't from the mediocrity of Global. It was the people. Not the people in the building but the people watching our news program. It was the relationship with the viewers I now realized that I missed the most. That connection with the audience had been part of my life for a long time.

I know some broadcasters hold the audience in contempt. They are on the air every night and consider themselves superior to the people they're talking too. I never felt that way. The audience was the entire reason for me doing my job. What was the point of doing a story if there was no one to tell it to? Never, in forty years, did I think I was talking into a vacuum. And viewers responded with many phone calls and letters.

Sometimes they praised me, such as May C. in Bedford who told me she could hardly wait for The Final Word because she felt I had the guts to say what many wouldn't and she thanked me for the excellent few minutes of truth.

Receiving a letter like that gave me an emotional boost. But, believe me, they weren't all complimentary.

A letter from Robert A. said I was beginning to sound like a radical with a dream of communism and that I should really learn to deliver an editorial without so much judgment and a little less condemnation. At the bottom of his letter Robert wrote, "My typing is as poor as Bruce's attitude."

You have to love that type of comment.

Ernest G. from Fredericton wrote a very critical letter regarding my comments on marketing boards. He told me I should spend a day on a dairy farm. All right, I admit it. I'm not a big fan of marketing boards and, of course, dairy farmers in particular didn't like that sort of talk.

I was never convinced the Savage government did the right thing in opening Nova Scotia to gambling. Today, with 50,000 problem gamblers in the province, I may have been right. When I refused to jump on the casino bandwagon in 1994, Creelman M. wrote that my Final Word comments were like something out of the 1930s anti-booze stance. And he told me I should give the casino issue a break.

Sometimes viewers wrote about certain words they picked up in the news. Kim G. from Greenwood, Nova Scotia, wanted to know when everyone but women started getting raped. She had picked up the comment of one man who, on the topic of the Shubie controversy, said, "We're being raped for every cent they can get." Kim was frustrated. She felt that at some point in time, society should no longer tolerate the graphic and strong word "rape" for anything but that sick crime against women.

Through much of the '90s gun control was in the news and I was always against what Allen Rock and the Liberal government were trying to do. As thousands of people predicted, the federal gun control legislation was a complete boondoggle, a billion-dollar waste of time and money. There are more shootings in places like Toronto and Montreal now than ever before. Gun control might have worked if it had tackled the problem of taking guns out of the hands of the criminal element but it didn't. It made PEI farmers register their goose guns but didn't have any impact on illegal weapons in the hands of hoodlums. I said so many times on the air and many viewers agreed. As Wayne B. of Debert, Nova Scotia, wrote, "We are not the criminals."

Homophobia was often rampant in this part of the world when I was on the air. I've always taken the view that minorities have the same rights as the rest of us. I'm happy to say as a society we are somewhat more lenient today than in 1995. I received more abuse over my support of minorities than anything else. Sometimes even critically worded letters were fair and very well-balanced.

Allan S. of Halifax wrote in response to my November '95 commentary in which I stated medical research had identified a gene that predisposes persons to homosexuality. He simply disagreed with me.

He said that rarely does a week go by that scientific literature does not identify a gene or some physiological marker that accounts for or explains a particular behaviour. Literature is full of such explanations on obesity, alcoholism, child molesters and compulsive gamblers. While there may be scientific explanations for aberrant behaviour, these explanations do not release the individual from personal responsibility. It is true that some of us have predispositions towards certain behaviours; to suggest that they are beyond our control and cannot be resisted is simply untrue. Society would be in a very sorry state if we did not on an individual basis consciously resist every temptation that we are confronted with.

He said I, as a prominent television personality in a position of great influence, should use that position to offer my viewing audience unbiased and balanced commentary and that the legal system already fosters the notion that personal responsibility is secondary to external factors, such as, "I cannot be held accountable for this crime because I was drunk." He asked me not to demean the office of my position with such nonsense.

Allan S. was much more correct than I was. It turned out the 1995 scientific finding was more theory than fact.

If I received a really nasty letter, I would find the writer, even if it took time away from other work. I once shocked a man who had written me a verbally abusive letter. He had signed his name but had not given his address. I tracked him down and, after his initial surprise, we ended by having a decent conversation.

Some of the letters were absolutely flattering, like the one from a viewer who said he had spent the previous forty years living everywhere from Labrador to south Florida, and had watched many program segments similar to The Final Word, such as Opinion, Manager's Word, Viewpoint, Footnote and so on. He commented that he truly enjoyed The Final Word because it was so to the point, current, well-spoken and relevant.

The commentary he was writing about concerned the deportation of two families, and he felt I was right in saying there was something wrong with the Canadian immigration system. He was a native of Holland and a Canadian by choice and identified with the fact that if immigrants have the ability to enrich this country they should be allowed to do so. He told me to keep up the good work and thanked me for a job well done.

As you can see, I had a lively, often animated relationship with viewers. It was that relationship I realized I missed that day walking away from Global, after seeing ten years worth of awards hidden away from the public and even most of the staff. It's that relationship I still miss today. But that's the only aspect of television I miss, the people who made it all worthwhile.

18

Parting Shots

Violence

For years the broadcast executives marched before regulatory agencies in both Canada and the United States and solemnly promised to curb violence in their programming. Then they did just the opposite.

A&E began as "The Arts and Entertainment Network," and they broadcast literary films and biographies of contributors to science, literature and society generally. Then they began a constant stream of crime shows and even Biography was only about mobsters. Their new catchphrase was "The Art of Entertainment." Now they run *The Sopranos* at 5:00 in the afternoon, just in time for the kiddies already home from school.

There is hardly a program in prime time television today that doesn't advise viewers to use their discretion before watching. That's a lot of discretion, certainly more than has ever been practised by any government, and certainly more than any government gives to citizens. If we could really be relied upon to demonstrate so much discretion, it wouldn't be necessary to have all the laws and regulations we have today. If people used discretion they wouldn't drive while talking on a cell phone or after consuming alcohol. After all, discretion means to be careful in how we act or speak. Making the discretionary suggestion on television is hollow and flimsy. The greatest abusers of discretion are the television executives who constantly thwart discretion for profit. If you watch

CTV for an evening you're constantly told (or warned) to practise discretion. Yet how much is practised in putting on violent cartoons such as Family Guy, where Stewie slaps, kicks and beats his dog with a towel rod until blood gushes out of the poor animal? The following week people are horrified in the Maritimes when a dog is hung from a tree.

People suggest that cartoons have always been violent and they point to *The Road Runner* as an example. But *The Road Runner* is of a lesser reality because the animals are drawn somewhat out of proportion. Even when Wyle E. Coyote falls over a cliff he's back again in the next frame. There is no blood or gore as when the perverted Stewie beats his dog to a bloody pulp. Television has tremendous influence and unfortunately it is not a very good one. Every survey reports children spend thousands of hours watching television during their impressionable years. You can often see the results.

There is another health issue with regard to the negativity of television. Have you noticed that many products advertised on television are actually not good for you? Take the time to jot down what sponsors and what products are being pushed at you. Artery-clogging Big Macs and all McDonald's competitors are there. So are substances that shower your home with chemicals to make it smell like wild flowers, except what you're inhaling may have unsuspected consequences. There are medicines, of course, from headache relief to stool softeners to remedies for erectile dysfunction.

"If your erection lasts more than four hours, don't enjoy it – rush to your doctor."

Not to mention the number of prescription drugs being pushed for everything – depression, anxiety, hair loss, sleep disorder and lovely things like bowel dysfunctions. At least now, prescription medications have to reveal heretofore secret side effects.

"Usage may cause swelling of the bladder, nosebleeds, sore throats and headaches. Some users may experience dizziness, vomiting, skin irritation and diarrhea."

Commercials that offer you great savings are always suspect. Television advertising is expensive. You're not only paying for the product but you're also paying for the high price of putting the product on TV. The customer always pays. There's nobody else.

Automotive commercials offer deals but have a lot of print on the screen that's impossible to read, even if you have 20-20 vision and are sitting very close to the TV. You can barely see it, let alone read it, but the advertiser and the broadcaster are complying with the law. It's the law and in this case the law is an ass. Advertisers and broadcasters are just using the loophole and it's high time somebody closed it. Yes, it's a swindle but a legal one and apparently nobody cares.

The other problem with commercials is their frequency. Broadcasters were recently given permission (can you believe it?) to increase the number of commercial minutes an hour. The problem now is that there are so many commercials, the plot of the program is often lost in a sea of meaningless messages. Viewers have to pick up the thread of the story every few minutes after a commercial break. For example, on the Women's Network, a two-hour movie can be three hours, interrupted sometimes every five minutes. It's another step in turning people off television. But that's not all.

Television commercials have lost their impact because their ability to convince has dissipated by overuse. Few people are influenced to purchase a product. Technology may take care of the problem of commercials and another form of support may be found. In England, television viewers have to pay an annual TV license fee. That may not work in Canada because of the smaller population, but I can tell you the British do some pretty good programs and you can enjoy them without being constantly bombarded by annoying ads for things you don't need or want.

Even entertaining commercials have lost their ability to influence. They may be funny or clever but that does not mean they are effective as selling tools. I like the Bud Light commercials in the Super Bowl and the little green lizard is cute in the Geico commercials. But I don't buy Bud Light and I don't have insurance with Geico. I enjoy their commercials but their ability to influence me has waned.

Nothing Important in Here

Former Live at 5 host Ron Kronstien has an acerbic wit. He was always grounded about the business. I was back in ATV for a book interview and Ron was showing me around. It had been several years since I had been in the building and there were many changes in people, props and certainly in the newsroom design. ATV News had done a complete makeover. They had retained the open newsroom concept but added glitzy graphics and high-tech backgrounds. To be honest, it was impressive and I remarked to Ron how cool the new look was and how high-tech and show-biz it appeared. Ron looked around at the lights and monitors and mused, "Yes, it's very impressive and there isn't a thing in here that's important." He wasn't referring to ATV specifically but about television generally. I knew exactly what he meant.

Bosses

I've been a boss and had bosses. It's more difficult being one than having one. Les Stoodley, the host of MITV's Noonhour, once said, "Bruce listens to everybody, but when the occasion merits, he has a nice way of telling employees to go to hell."

I've had some good bosses and some clunkers. Jim Purvis of CKY in Winnipeg and Dick Prat of ATV Halifax were the two best bosses I had in the business. They were entirely different men in both approach and personality. But they both gave me a huge comfort level. I suppose we all use different criteria for evaluating a boss. Personally, I rate honesty as a higher value than most other traits. I like a boss who tells you the truth even when it hurts and a boss who will go to bat for you. After all, personal loyalty works both ways. A boss who is loyal to you is more apt to receive loyalty in return. Jim was taken by cancer way too early and Dick is now selling real estate.

I know it sounds quaint today to be talking of loyalty to a boss or to a company. Loyalty is another trait dropping down the sinkhole of time, following the TV test pattern, the film camera and the IBM electric typewriter. To be truthful, for the manner in which companies treat their employees today, they don't deserve much loyalty.

Finally, I want to write a few words on what makes a great reporter. Certainly in television it's the ability to blend words and pictures, but that's only part of it. Journalism is really intuitive and that's true regardless of what medium you're working in. A top-flight journalist has the ability to see a news story in any circumstances of a given situation. It's the gift of going to a news conference, listening to the speaker and seeing the story behind what they are talking about. It's the ability to find news, to discover a good story. That's a sixth sense or, as I already said, it's intuitive.

It's been a fabulous career and my life is packed with great memories. I was there for the last golden era of radio and the best years of television. In 2004, Helen and I moved back to our hometown of Parrsboro. We have a little house by the sea, gardens to tend and books to write. So let me leave you with the sign off I used every night.

"Thanks for watching."